THE
HOLISTIC
CAT

THE HOLISTIC CAT

A Complete Guide to Wellness for a Healthier, Happier Cat

JENNIFER A. COSCIA, NC

Foreword by Don Hamilton, DVM

North Atlantic Books
Berkeley, California

Published by
North Atlantic Books
P.O. Box 12327
Berkeley, California 94712

Cover photo by Cheri Audett
Cover and book design by Suzanne Albertson
Printed in the United States of America

Excerpt from *Small Animal Practice (Current Veterinary, Therapy XI)*, 11th edition, by Robert W. Kirk and John D. Bonagura, copyright 1992 by Harcourt. Used by permission from Elsevier.

Data from *Springhouse Nurse's Drug Guide 2005*
The author sent numerous requests for permission to Lippincott Williams & Wilkins, but did not receive a response. If you have any information, please contact North Atlantic Books.

The Holistic Cat: A Complete Guide to Wellness for a Healthier, Happier Cat is sponsored by the Society for the Study of Native Arts and Sciences, a nonprofit educational corporation whose goals are to develop an educational and cross-cultural perspective linking various scientific, social, and artistic fields; to nurture a holistic view of arts, sciences, humanities, and healing; and to publish and distribute literature on the relationship of mind, body, and nature.

North Atlantic Books' publications are available through most bookstores. For further information, visit our Web site at www.northatlanticbooks.com or call 800-733-3000.

Library of Congress Cataloging-in-Publication Data

Coscia, Jennifer A.
    The holistic cat : a complete guide to wellness for a healthier, happier cat / Jennifer A. Coscia ; foreword by Don Hamilton.
       p. cm.
    Summary: "Offers information on how to raise a cat in a healthy, stress-free, and safe environment, with a focus on disease prevention and including rescue stories and photos"—Provided by publisher.
    ISBN 978-1-55643-766-3
    1. Cats. 2. Cats—Health. 3. Cats—Diseases—Alternative treatment. 4. Holistic veterinary medicine. I. Title.
    SF447.C67 2008
    636.8'083—dc22

2008026543

1 2 3 4 5 6 7 8 9 SHERIDAN 14 13 12 11 10 09

This book is dedicated to Baby, Silver, Wilma, Bob, Casey, Stormy, Hope, and all the other cats and kittens that shared, enriched, and inspired my life. The time that we are given with these wonderful, beautiful creatures is truly precious. And the little amount of time that we are blessed with never seems to be enough. Live and cherish each day as if it were your last.

Many Blessings,
Jennifer

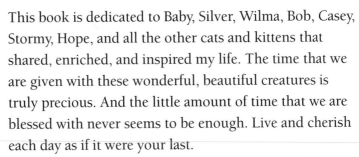

ACKNOWLEDGMENTS

I would like to express my heartfelt gratitude to the many colleagues, friends, and family that have helped make this book possible.

First of all, my husband, Michael, for all the support he has given to me throughout the years. I wish to thank him for his patience and understanding and, most of all, the compassion and love he has shown toward the animals that we have taken into our care. He is truly the strength, both physical and emotional, behind The Animal Rescue and Adoption Agency, Inc. (TARAA).

My heartfelt gratitude goes out to my literary agency, Waterside Productions, for having faith in this project from the very beginning.

I would also like to thank Carolyn Fogarty for playing such an intrinsic role in the formation of TARAA; without her help it would not have been possible.

My undying gratitude goes out to the real heroes at TARAA, our foster care parents: Lynne Highfill, Michelle and Tim Mercurio, Shirley and Sara McIntyre, Marie Harper, Heather Deane and Carrie Jackson, the Connelly Family, Jane Akre and her daughter Alex, and all the other families that have opened their homes and hearts to the many cats and kittens in need of a soft place to land.

Doc and his staff (who have chosen to remain anonymous) have a very special place in my heart for without their medical intervention many of the animals that TARAA has taken in over the years would not have survived.

I would also like to mention a personal thank you to Dr. Stephen Hart for his assistance with the wildlife TARAA has taken in. His compassion for these animals should be commended, especially for his work with raccoons and feral cats. For his medical expertise and the priceless education he has blessed me with, I will be forever thankful.

And finally, I would like to thank Petco, especially Connie LeBlanc and her team at the Jacksonville Beach location, for their fund-raising efforts as well as their assistance in helping TARAA place hundreds of homeless animals into homes with loving families. And to all the wonderful, caring families that have adopted these pets—I thank you with all my heart!

Contents

did not need to read far into Jennifer's book to grasp the size of her heart; her dedication to cats and the loving effort she devotes to homeless cats are more than admirable. I'd say she is a saint, and while she is surely not alone in this compassionate work, she is also far from average in giving her time to others in need. I honor her for this alone.

Fortunately for the rest of us, she has channeled some of her energy into this book—a warmly written guidebook for providing your cat with the best life possible in this modern world, a world that is not always kind to its inhabitants. Jennifer covers not only such basics as nutrition, supplementation, and medical care, but also general cat care from a caring, loving perspective. Her goal, obviously, is to extend her reach farther than her physical body allows by offering good suggestions that can help cats everywhere lead a healthier, happier life. And I think she will succeed with this goal. Our congested world is often a frightening, difficult place for cats, and we owe them the best homes and care we can give them to help offset some of the stresses.

I don't necessarily agree with all recommendations here. I think there are potentially serious problems with microchips, for example, and I am a believer in not confining cats (indoor or outdoor) in most circumstances, knowing they prefer freedom to safety. But these are not clear-cut issues by any means—in some locations (though not most), it is better to keep cats indoors, and microchips do help reunite animals and guardians. Truth is relative, so these minor disagreements in no way detract from the value Jennifer has provided in this, her greater offering to the cat family. She has clearly spent hours and hours seeking the best information available and putting it together so you can give your feline companions a better life. There are a lot of good suggestions in here, and there are stories to demonstrate her viewpoint—stories that also may lead you to rethink some of your previous assumptions about cat care. Altogether, these produce a book that is fun to read while providing new ideas you can use. If you want to improve your cat's (and, therefore, your own) life, this book can help you on that journey.

—DON HAMILTON, DVM, author of
Homeopathic Care for Cats and Dogs: Small Doses for Small Animals

INTRODUCTION

Over the years I have seen too many homeless, diseased, abused, and neglected animals, the majority of which were cats and kittens. Writing a book on disease prevention and wellness for cats is my way of giving back to all of you who have opened your hearts and homes to receive these very special creatures. I also wish to share with you my passion for helping to eradicate the ever-growing problem of homeless, unwanted pets. I truly believe that, through community effort, education, spaying/neutering, and adoption programs, this mission will succeed.

I am a holistic nutritional consultant and author of *The Fat Elimination and Detox Program (FED): A Holistic Approach to Disease Prevention and Weight Loss*. I also own and operate a rescue and adoption agency called The Animal Rescue and Adoption Agency, Inc. (TARAA). With the aid of Petco Corporation, we have placed hundreds of homeless animals into deserving homes. TARAA is a non-profit/no-kill organization that relies heavily on a foster care program and outside donations.

It is only recently, after the loss of two of my adult cats, that I began to question conventional veterinary medicine. They both died of cardiomyopathy (heart disease), which was possibly vaccine related. Baby, a handsome white domestic-shorthair male, was only four years old; and Silver, a silver Maine coon mix, was barely two. These cats were far too young to die. Baby was vaccinated annually, and Silver had received all his vaccines just three months before he died. Their deaths prompted my research into vaccine-related illnesses in cats, and I will share my findings with you later in this book.

I have been involved with animal rescue (of cats in particular) for the past seventeen years, and I must tell you I have seen it all. I've seen cats hurled from cars, thrown from bridges, burned alive (and survived), ripped apart by dogs, drowned in pools, and born with severe deformities including backward feet. I even had two five-week-old kittens who had ridden from Miami to Jacksonville in the wheel well of an eighteen-wheeler. I have rescued kittens that were born in walls, in condemned buildings, inside a flooded drainpipe under a road, on a boat, and even in the engine of a truck in a wrecking yard. As part of TARAA's mission to reduce the numbers of unwanted or homeless cats, we've dwindled down several feral cat colonies by adopting out the adoptable cats and spaying/neutering the remaining ones. So far, the journey has been bittersweet, but we have had more joy than sorrow, I am happy to say. My husband says that the best therapy for anything that troubles you is to sit on the floor in a room full of kittens. Their antics will surely put a smile on your face.

Growing up, my family always had a bit of a zoo—at one point we had six indoor cats and three dogs. I am sure we vaccinated them at some point in their lives but nowhere near to the extent of the recommended vaccine protocols of today—veterinarians now recommend up to three to four vaccines before a kitten reaches four months of age. (I have personally buried many kittens that became sick after immunization, probably because they were immune-suppressed to begin with and never should have been vaccinated. I will discuss this topic more later on.) Most of my family's pets lived well into their teens. I can recall very few visits to the vet because our animals just didn't get sick—at least not until they were approaching their senior years—unlike the pets of today.

Many animals these days suffer chronic conditions like allergy problems, joint problems, intestinal difficulties, kidney and urinary tract issues, thyroid disorders, heart disease, and, finally, cancer. In fact, one of the leading diseases in cats is cancer, and I am shocked each time I hear from adopters that they just had to put their cat down due to this disease. Cringing, I ask them how old the cat was and their reply is heart breaking. You would expect that the cat had been in its senior years, but too often I hear it was less than nine years old. I also frequently hear that a cat died of old-age-related illness at the age of ten or twelve years, while according to the Humane Society the average life expectancy for an indoor cat in the United States is supposed to be seventeen plus years.

What has changed so drastically in the last twenty or so years? And why do we see so much disease today? My theory is that the overuse of vaccines and drugs in veterinary care, along with the multitude of chemicals and contaminants that are added to pet foods and our water supply, is slowly killing our cats. Diet too plays a crucial role in the health and life expectancy of our cats. The Humane Society also stated that a cat today lives more than double the life expectancy of that of a cat from eighty years ago. But take a look at the state our country was in during the 1930s and 1940s. Times were tough; we were in the midst of a depression followed by war, and food was scarce for all—let alone cats. So, logically speaking, cats today should live at least double the life expectancy of the felines of yesteryear as food is no longer scarce.

While studying for my nutrition degree, I had the opportunity to take a few classes on the care of domestic pets, and one of the required readings was *Homeopathic Care for Cats and Dogs* by Don Hamilton, DVM. This book opened my eyes to the epidemic of chronic illness and the overuse of vaccines in pets today. Since then, I have seen firsthand the truths I learned in my courses, and I have an overwhelming need to share this information with you.

I must also say that I am not writing this book to "bash" conventional medicine. On the contrary, actually, I will praise conventional medicine and give credit where credit is due; however, I believe that conventional medicine combined with holistic medicine is the best form of health care for your cat. This unique combination is called complementary medicine and simply means that each complements the other (I will explain complementary medicine in more detail throughout this book).

You obviously care a great deal about your pet; otherwise, you probably wouldn't have purchased this book. With this in mind, I will tell you how I got started on this path and share with you my experiences.

The First Rescue

In June of 1990 I was riding a bicycle around our Long Island neighborhood with my daughter, Arielle. As we rode down a street in a nearby development where a vacant wooded lot remained, we noticed a large box in the middle of the lot and immediately decided to investigate. The box contained only a dirty food dish, an empty bowl (I assumed it was once used for water), and a filthy towel. Suddenly, Arielle shrieked with joy as she spotted seven young kittens playing on a nearby log. I didn't see a mama cat anywhere nearby, so I deduced that the kittens had been abandoned without their mother. This was to be my first rescue/trapping experience.

The kittens were scared to death and all of them scattered into the woods as we approached, but, over the next two days, we worked hard to successfully trap every one. Though they appeared to be in pretty good shape, I knew we couldn't keep them since we already had a bit of a zoo. Thus, I called the North Shore Animal League in Port Washington, New York. They were very helpful as they already had me on file from my previous adoption of a wonderful dog named Frisco. They advised me to socialize the kittens—which meant to make them friendly—and then bring them to their shelter for placement in their adoption program. Naturally, we fell in love with all the kittens, but, in particular, a beautiful Russian blue we called Smokey. We ended up keeping just Smokey and later found out that all remaining kittens went to good homes within one week (thanks to the North Shore Animal League).

Over the years we continued our animal rescue efforts in several states, and our zoo rapidly expanded so that our pets outgrew our home. Because my husband Michael is an engineer, we moved quite a bit, and with Arielle going into high school, we made the decision to put down roots in Jacksonville, Florida. We began planning the home of our dreams. Our new house was completed in the fall of 2002.

Shortly after moving into our new house, Michael was doing some finishing work and needed some additional supplies. He headed up to the local hardware store, and, after he accidentally locked his keys in his truck, I was called to his rescue. As I turned into the parking area, which is bordered by woods, I saw a beautiful red fox standing in the middle of the street. It ran over to my car, looked right at me, and then disappeared into the woods. I was curious to know where it went, so I gave Michael the spare set of keys and asked him to meet me behind the store near the woods. As I approached the place where the fox had disappeared, I saw twenty heads pop up all along the grass and farther into the woods. Twenty-three cats and kittens, to be exact, and one fox all waiting to be fed. They were starving and sick, and three of the kittens had upper respiratory infection with severe conjunctivitis. So, back into the store we went to purchase a trap, and that night we caught the three sick kittens.

This was my first feral colony rescue and, boy, was I in for an education. I decided that night that the word "feral" not only meant wild but could also mean ferocious. How could two grown adult human beings be absolutely terrified of a tiny fur ball with fangs and claws? This particular fur ball was a Himalayan we named Gabby, and she literally climbed the bathroom walls and doorjambs. She made the Tasmanian devil look like an angel—we had our work cut out for us.

Michael and I were overwhelmed by the task laid out before us. With twenty more cats and kittens remaining in the colony, it was going to cost a lot of money to take care of these animals. So Michael took it upon himself to do an online search for help and came up with an organization here in Jacksonville called The Bear Foundation—a nonprofit agency that would have funds available to help us with our

Gabriella—with time, Gabby's manner improved, and today she is a beautiful five-year-old and permanent resident in our home.

mission. We contacted The Bear Foundation, and they immediately took us under their wing. They educated us about the TAR program, which stands for trap, alter (spay/neuter), and return. Once spayed/neutered, the cats that were too feral would be returned back to the area they came from. Those that were eligible for adoption would be placed into the adoption program and shown every weekend at a local pet store.

I initially had a problem with spaying/neutering a young kitten. I felt it was cruel—that is, until I learned the statistics: UC Davis reports that several million cats and kittens born in the wild are killed each year by cars alone. These numbers do not include deaths caused by disease, predators, and human cruelty. So, needless to say, I soon changed my views on spaying/neutering.

We agreed to foster our own rescued cats and kittens in our home until they were adopted (I'll never forget little Raphael, a sweet orange tabby and the first kitten from the colony to get adopted; it was very difficult to give him up—I remember crying all the way home). The first time I participated in the adoptions, I had to excuse myself and go out to my car where I cried for twenty minutes. I am not a crybaby sort of person, but my initial impression of these adoptions was one of great sorrow. It broke my heart to see so many unwanted pets. Cats and kittens of all ages were in cages, and it really affected me. There were over fifty of them there that day and all of them vying for attention, as if they knew that this was their chance to go to a real home.

To this day, I have a problem keeping cats in cages, which is why our agency runs a foster care program rather than a traditional shelter. This program also helps to cut down on the spread of disease and gives the animals a chance to gain socialization skills with other animals, children, and their caregivers. I knew from that first adoption day experience that I would do all I could for these cats and kittens. I also knew I was in it for the long haul.

It took us about a year to reduce the colony to just three resident cats. Their names are Tommy, Prissy, and Blackie, and we have continued to take care of them on a daily basis. All of the other cats and kittens, including the pregnant mothers and their babies, were given medical care and adopted out to good homes. Unfortunately, however, The Bear Foundation folded halfway through our efforts, making it very difficult for us to continue our work. In spite of this setback, I was able to make special veterinary care arrangements with a local veterinarian who we all call Doc. Doc and his staff have gone above and beyond the call of duty to help us out. I am and will be forever grateful for all their support.

Eventually, I branched out on my own, forming The Animal Rescue and Adoption Agency, Inc. (TARAA). As I mentioned earlier, we have had our share of joy and heartache. The joy of knowing that an animal is no longer vulnerable and alone on the street or fending for itself in the woods is what keeps the rescue going. Each time a kitty is placed in the arms of a worthy adopter, the reward makes all we must endure worth it. On the other hand, losing cats and kittens to disease takes a little piece of our hearts every time. We have lost too many of these angels over the years.

With this book, I want to share the experience and knowledge I have gained in both nutrition and animal rescue. *The Holistic Cat* was written to give you easy-to-follow guidelines on how to prolong and enhance the life of your cat. With education we will overcome ignorance, and without ignorance all things are possible.

Silver II

CHAPTER ONE

Holistic Nutrition—
For the Life of Your Cat

Why Holistic Nutrition?

I first want to clarify exactly what the word "holistic" means. If you were to look it up in the dictionary, it would say it is a philosophy based on the principle that everything in nature, such as complete individuals and other complete organisms, functions as a complete unit that cannot be reduced to the sum of its parts. In other words, a holistic approach to health care would mean that the practitioner would look at the whole body, not just individual parts or symptoms. When used to describe food, the word holistic refers to the whole food instead of the parts thereof. In this book, we are going to discuss the whole cat. We will consider every aspect of a cat's life in order to fully understand how to give them all exactly what they need for a longer, happier, healthier life.

As a holistic nutritionist, I firmly believe that you are what you eat, and I have proven it numerous times with my clients. When you feed your body at a cellular level, meaning healthy food that's chock-full of nutrients, your body will perform the way it was designed to. An unhealthy diet consisting of nutrient-void food, like most processed food, will not feed or energize your cells (your body). The same holds true for your pets. Did you know that dietary deficiencies are one of the factors of chronic disease and that one single nutrient deficiency can wreak all sorts of havoc within the body? For example, a deficiency in taurine, which is a very important amino acid, has been linked to cardiomyopathy (heart disease) and blindness in cats. I will discuss more about deficiencies later on in this chapter.

Many world-renowned veterinarians agree that a dry food diet is one of the worst things you can feed your pets. Most dry foods are seriously lacking in natural vital nutrients and are loaded with preservatives, by-products, and artificial flavors and colors. Veterinarians

3

like Richard Pitcairn and Don Hamilton recommend that you feed your cat a diet that is rich in raw meats, fresh-cooked grains and vegetables, and a few supplements just to balance the diet out. However, watch out for those fancy so-called natural health pet foods that are loaded with things that cats should *not* eat. One food that I recently purchased claimed to be the best food for cats and contained good organic grains and free-range meats. But then they added dried mangoes, bananas, apples, and raisins—my cats threw up and had diarrhea for a week! What cat in the wild ever consumed dried bananas or mangoes?

Cats have extremely sensitive stomachs and can easily develop allergies and food sensitivities, which will ultimately jeopardize the integrity of their guts, as well as cause a whole slew of other health problems. Cats are carnivores and meat should be the main staple in their diet. A high-grain, high-carbohydrate vegetarian diet is the worst kind of diet for your cat. Such a low-protein diet will only rob from the cat's own tissue what the body needs. Realistically speaking, choose a good natural food that has no preservatives, artificial colors and flavors, fillers, or synthetic supplements. I will give you a detailed list of what not to buy later on in this chapter.

The Pottenger Study

There was a very interesting study carried out by Dr. Francis Marion Pottenger that was simply called *Pottenger's Cats: A Study in Nutrition*. It was first published in 1939. Between the years 1932 and 1942, Dr. Pottenger studied two groups of cats that were put on two different diets. He fed one group a raw food diet that consisted of meat, bones, milk, and cod liver oil. The second group received cooked food, homogenized milk, and cod liver oil. The cats on the entirely raw diet thrived. They were completely healthy and rarely needed veterinary care. However, the second group—the cats on the cooked-food diet— were amazingly similar health-wise to the regular domestic cats we see today that suffer from mouth and gum problems, thyroid disorders, bladder inflammation, kidney disease, and poor immune function. Over a period of three generations, the cats on the cooked-food diet continued to deteriorate and were no longer able to reproduce. When the cats in this group were put on the same raw food diet as the other group, it took four more generations for the cats to totally recover from the physical effects of the cooked-food diet. There certainly was a lot to be learned from this study, and it's a shame that it has not made a difference in the preparation of most commercial pet foods and the overall diet of cats today.

Pros and Cons of a Raw Food Diet

Now with that said, feeding your cats a raw food diet doesn't mean you have to go out and catch rodents, fish, or chickens. It would benefit your cats greatly if you added just a little raw meat and vegetables into their diet gradually. This will ensure that you don't cause them intestinal upset. While you are preparing your own meals, cut off some of the meat (before cooking), add some lightly steamed vegetables such as carrots, peas, broccoli, or green beans, and mash everything together. I lightly steam the vegetables to retain nutritive values and to ease consumption. Next, add cooked brown rice, puree all the ingredients together, and place the mixture in individual containers to freeze. I will list separately the supplements I recommend for cats in the next section.

A very important note to remember is to *never* give onions to your cats—onions are extremely toxic to felines. A small amount of garlic is actually good for them and is also a great flea deterrent, especially when given with brewer's yeast because of the high B vitamin content. However, too much garlic can be lethal to young cats and kittens as garlic destroys red blood cells. More positively, did you know that vitamin B3 (niacin) is a natural repellent for mosquitoes when taken orally? This applies to both felines and humans.

PRO—improved health: I did give my household pets a home-cooked diet for a few months to see if it would make a difference, and I have to say that it did. I noticed shinier coats, fewer hair ball issues, less smell in the litter box, and overall improved health. Below is the recipe I used.

The Holistic Cat Natural Foods Recipe for Wellness

Organic Ingredients:

> 1 lb. ground organic turkey chop (Shelton's is a good brand)
> 4 oz. organic liver or kidney
> ¼ cup cooked barley
> ¼ cup cooked brown rice
> 1 organic egg
> ¼ jar baby food peas
> ¼ jar baby food carrots
> 1 tablespoon Solid Gold Sea Meal
> 1 pinch granulated pure garlic
> 1 tablespoon flaxseed oil
> 1 tablespoon brewer's yeast
> 500 mg crushed bromelain (digestive enzyme)
> 500 mg crushed L-lysine
> 500 mg taurine (capsule)
> 1 tablespoon Solgar's Bone Meal
> 500 mg buffered vitamin C (capsule)
> 200 mg vitamin E (oil)

Preparation:

> Put all ingredients into a blender and blend until smooth.
> Makes 4½ cups.

Divide this recipe into individual servings the size of a sausage patty and freeze. The evening before you feed your cat, put a serving in the refrigerator so it will thaw by morning. Do not serve cold and do not microwave. Let it come up to room temperature before serving. For extra flavor and nutrients, I also add some Bragg's Amino Acid Spray, which is similar to soy sauce in flavor. The cats seem to like it.

It took awhile to transition my cats from canned food to this home-made healthy concoction. They didn't like it in the beginning; how-ever, they eventually caught on when they realized that nothing else was on the menu.

CON—time-consuming: As a complete diet this regime became time intensive and impossible for me to keep up with. By the time I got home from work, planned and prepared dinner for my family, and cleaned up, I was exhausted. Finding the time to prepare the pet's food seemed impossible. So I have now gone back to a good natural canned food; however, I add greens, flaxseed oil, and the rest of the supplements I mentioned in the recipe. As a nutritionist, I know that heat and processing destroy vital nutrients (I will go more in depth on this in the next section). I chose to add these supplements to ensure that my cats were getting what they needed just in case the nutrients were destroyed in the canning process. During the day I give them a natural, wholesome brand of dry food. This particular dry-food manufacturer only uses whole foods and their ingredients contain no fillers, by-products, artificial flavors, or colors. Touted for containing human-grade ingredients, the only thing that could improve its quality would be the inclusion of organic products.

If you are going to give your cat dry food, you must make sure there is an ample supply of fresh, clean water. And in this section I hope to change your mind about dry-food-only diets in general. As I pointed out earlier, most holistic veterinarians will tell you that such a diet is a health disaster waiting to happen. Drop a kibble of cat food into a glass of water. Notice how it expands as it is saturated with water. When your cat eats this food, the same thing happens in his stom-ach. He will always be slightly dehydrated from this diet. He will drink more water, causing more wear and tear on his urinary tract system and, most importantly, his kidneys. He will also have a good chance

Prissy basking in the sun

of developing diabetes, and, if he is an indoor-only cat, he may have multiple urinary tract infections throughout his life. The traditional dry-food-only diet is excessive in carbohydrate content—and these are not the good carbs. I have found all this to be true. Out of all the cats in our care, there are two that outright refuse to eat wet food: Toby and Prissy who have had numerous urinary tract infections over the years. I finally got Prissy to eat wet food, and she hasn't had urinary issues in a little over a year now.

CON—contamination: If you do decide to give your cat raw meats, make sure they are organic or free-range/roam meats. Always rinse the meat in a light bleach solution of one tablespoon of bleach to one gallon of water. This will get rid of any bacteria from the packaging process. Buying organic meat will also ensure that you and your cat are not getting any of the added antibiotics of growth hormones that commercial meats are usually loaded with.

Here are a few facts for you to mull over the next time you consider buying cheap commercial-brand pet food. Each year approximately 116,000 mammals and over fifteen million birds are slaughtered. After slaughter 325,000 carcasses are discarded, and more than 5.5 million body parts are cut away because they are diseased. Annually, 140,000 tons of poultry parts are condemned primarily due to cancer. The diseased animals or parts thereof, which include pigs, cows, horses, chickens, turkeys, ducks, and, unfortunately in some states, cats and dogs, are processed into—you guessed it—pet food. The meat that is determined as unfit for human consumption is sold and rendered down. It is then sold to pet food manufacturers to use in their pet food and livestock feed. Rendering is a cheap, easy way to dispose of euthanized pets or pets that are brought into the veterinary clinic already deceased. If you wish to learn more about this horrific practice, see Ann N. Martin's *Foods Pets Die For: Shocking Facts About Pet Food.*

PRO—homemade foods contain only good ingredients: One of the best things about a homemade, raw diet is that you know exactly what goes into it. You don't have to worry about your cat consuming harmful or diseased ingredients. Below is a list of chemical additives you should avoid at all costs and this goes for treats as well. You can find these items listed on the labels of some of the most popular brands of pet food products:

- *Propylene glycol* (an ingredient in antifreeze)—used to keep food moist and inhibit bacterial growth. Under the "Federal Food, Drug, and Cosmetics Act," the FDA specifically states that, in their Code of Federal Regulations 21 CFR 582, "Propylene Glycol is considered Generally Recognized As Safe (GRAS) except for use in cat food." The FDA also says that the use of propylene glycol in or on cat food causes the feed to be adulterated, and, therefore, using this chemical in cat food is a direct violation under Code 21 CFR 589.1001. For more information on the safety of food additives, visit www.fda.gov.

- *Potassium sorbate*—a preservative that is chemically similar to fat.
- *High fructose corn syrup* (linked to the prevalence of diabetes)—used to keep products moist and add a sweet taste.
- *Propyl gallate*—slows the process of spoilage but causes liver damage.
- *Ethoxyquin*—a common preservative originally used for the production of rubber; it causes major health problems.
- *Ammoniated glycyrrhizin*—a sweetener and a potent drug that needs further investigation for safety.
- *Sodium nitrite*—produces powerful carcinogenic (cancer-causing) substances called nitrosamines.
- *Butylated hydroxytoluene (BHT)*—has been known to cause liver damage, metabolic stress, fetal abnormalities, and a serum cholesterol increase.
- Many of the following coloring additives are considered carcinogenic (cancer-causing): red no. 3, red no. 40, yellow no. 5 and 6, blue no. 1 and 2.

You must learn to look at food labels not only for your pets' sake, but also for the sake of you and your family because some of these same additives are in the food humans eat as well. Most of the cheap commercial pet foods that you can purchase from your local grocery store contain these harmful chemicals and cancer-causing dyes. Do you think your cat really cares about what color his food is? Pet food manufacturers create their food shapes, sizes, and colors based on what they think *we* would like, since *we* are the caregivers and the ones purchasing the food. The cats don't make that choice. This also goes for the packaging and name choices of individual flavors. Honestly, which would you prefer—a plain can that says "fish" on it, or a well-dressed can with a flavor of "Ocean Whitefish and Tuna

Fillets in Gravy"? The power of marketing is amazing.

Remember earlier when I said cancer was one of the leading killers of cats? It is not surprising that you truly are what you eat: Chemical additives cause the depletion of vital nutrients and energy as well as toxic accumulation within the tissues. So think twice about what's in the food you're feeding your cat.

According to J. Robert Hatherill, PhD, author of *Eat to Beat Cancer,* there are over seventy thousand chemicals in use today. Thousands more are added annually and we can now detect over six hundred chemicals in our bodies that were not present in the year 1900. Chemicals are found in our food and water supplies, the air we breathe, and the very chair you are sitting on, and chemicals make up just about everything around you. Is it any wonder that we and our pets are so unhealthy? Be sure to choose a good natural cat food with no by-products, and be wary of things like meat by-products, poultry by-product meal, chicken by-products, dried animal digest, liver glandular meal, dried liver digest, and fish meal. I am happy to report that, after investigating the ingredients in most of the better commercial pet foods, I did not find many of the harmful chemicals I mentioned previously. Also, as a reminder, keep in mind that a lot of what goes into pet food has been rejected for human consumption. Now, there are certainly things our cats eat that we ourselves wouldn't eat, such as lizards, bugs, and other live food. My point is that, if food has been rejected for our consumption, then it shouldn't be fit for animal consumption either, especially if it is rancid or riddled with cancer. Do you think the food we've been feeding our pets has contributed to their ill health? I know it has; however, it is just one of the many problems associated with cats and chronic disease.

Supplemental Support

You can dramatically improve your pets' health by supplementing the diet with vital nutrients. Earlier we discussed the Pottenger study;

however, we didn't talk about why the cooked food diet was so debilitating. Well, here it is in a nutshell—food processing. The term "processed food" means that the food has been altered from its original state (such as in cooking). When we cook food, we lose most of the valuable properties in the food. Enzymes are destroyed and vital nutrients are lost. This was the case in the Pottenger study. The amino acid taurine, which is vital to felines for maintaining heart health, is only found in the tissue (meat) of animals. Later it was discovered that 52 percent of the taurine in baked meat was lost, and a whopping 79 percent was lost during the boiling process. Cooked (processed) meat seriously lacks vital nutrients that are needed to maintain health.

In the past many commercial cat foods were extremely deficient in taurine, but now taurine is added back in to the food. However, I can't get a straight answer as to when this happens in the process. In other words, is the taurine that is added being destroyed again by the baking process? This uncertainty is the main reason that I add taurine a few times a week to my cats' diet. Cats cannot synthesize this amino acid on their own; therefore, it has to come directly from their diet. There seems to be a lot of controversy regarding the proper amount per cat, but the general consensus is 20–50 mg daily, depending on the weight of the cat. For therapeutic reasons such as eye problems or cardiac ailments, cats can have up to 125 mg daily. I've known some holistic veterinarians who will even double this for an acute phase problem.

There are quite a few supplements that I recommend and use on a daily basis. I will give you an overview of these supplements later on as well as some supplement formulas for specific ailments. For now, here are some of my favorites and why they are so important:

- *Flaxseed oil*—flaxseed oil has a wealth of medicinal properties. The many health benefits include protection against heart disease, stroke, and diabetes; anticarcinogenic activity against tumors; aid in the treatment of arthritis, asthma, and inflammatory disease; and normalization of blood sugar. Flaxseed oil also aids in fat metabolism, increases vitality, improves immune function, protects against cold weather, and improves function of the adrenals, reproductive system, and brain. It is also used to improve certain psychiatric behavior disorders and has anticarcinogenic, antifungal, and antiviral properties.

- *Calcium/magnesium/phosphorus/vitamin D*—these four power-house supplements are needed for bone and dental health, cell growth, and prevention of cancer, heart disease, osteoporosis, and kidney stones.

- *Lecithin* (also called phosphatidylcholine)—an important form of the fats called phospholipids. Lecithin's many benefits include protection against damage to cells by oxidation, prevention of heart disease, liver support, and lowering of cholesterol. Lecithin has also been used to treat arteriosclerosis and bipolar depression disorder as well as improve brain function, energy levels, and fat metabolism. Lecithin aids those suffering from chronic fatigue syndrome, AIDS, herpes, and other immune disorders. Lecithin actually works as a general detoxifier for the body by decongesting the liver of excess fats.

- *Spirulina*—a microalgae that has many healing properties. It provides a wide variety of nutrients to support cellular metabolism, naturally increase energy levels, and improve immune function. Naturally alkaline, spirulina also helps neutralize excess acidity.

- *Acid-free vitamin C powder* (buffered)—vitamin C is one of the most powerful antioxidants, and it is required for over three hundred metabolic functions within the body including the growth and repair of tissue, the functioning of the adrenals, and the production of anti-stress hormones and interferon (an important immune system protein). There is documented research that proves vitamin C's effect on the reduction of asthmatic symptoms and protection against chronic diseases like cancer and cardiovascular disease. It has also been shown to help fight off bacterial and viral infections as well as prevent the formation of cataracts. Vitamin C enhances immunity, increases the absorption of iron, aids in the elimination of toxic substances such as heavy metals, and promotes the healing of burns and wounds. Vitamin C works synergistically (together) with vitamins A (beta-carotene) and E.

- *Vitamin B6* (pyridoxine)—a drastically underrated vitamin as far as health properties go. B6 is actually involved in more bodily functions than any other nutrient. Here's why: B6 is foremost a warrior in the war on cancer and heart disease. B6 inhibits the absorption of homocysteine, which attacks the heart muscle, so it plays an important role in preventing cardiomyopathy. It is also touted for its ability to prevent kidney stones, treat asthma and arthritis, and act as a mild diuretic. When used with vitamin C and L-lysine, B6 prevents herpes virus outbreaks and effectively fights this virus

- *Brewer's yeast*—known as nature's wonder food and is certainly deserving of that title. It is an excellent source of all the major B vitamins (except B12). It also contains sixteen amino acids, fourteen (and possibly more) minerals, and many other vitamins. Health benefits include improving brain and immune function as well as combatting fatigue, diarrhea, and cancer.

- *Garlic*—did you know that Hippocrates (the father of medicine) had over two thousand medicinal recipes that included garlic? Garlic helps lower blood pressure, thins the blood (which reduces the risk of clotting), lowers serum cholesterol levels, supports the immune system, and serves as nature's most prized antibiotic. It is also antifungal, antibacterial, antiviral, and good for the heart, colon, joints (when arthritic), and circulation. This powerful supplement is also a great flea deterrent.

- *L-lysine*—when taken with vitamin C, L-lysine appears to help relieve symptoms of the heart condition angina pectoris. It has also been used to treat sores caused by the herpes simplex and herpes zoster viruses. Additionally, L-lysine prevents bone loss and improves immune function.
- *Taurine*—deters heart disease, diabetes, eye disorders, and liver diseases such as hepatitis.
- *Bromelain*—great for reducing inflammation, aiding digestion, and speeding up the healing process of wounds. It is also a digestive enzyme that helps break down proteins.
- *MSM* (methylsulfonylmethane)—a naturally occurring organic sulfur compound, MSM is needed for optimum health. Excellent for the coat, skin, and nails as well as allergy, pain, and inflammation relief, MSM is a promoter of intestinal and immune health. It should be given to cats after surgery or after a regimen of medication as it helps to detoxify the body at a cellular level.

As you can see, there is a lot to be gained when you incorporate these powerful supplements into your cat's diet. These supplements together help ward off many ailments and maintain heart, brain, kidney, liver, digestive, urinary tract, and bone health, as well as—and most importantly—your cat's overall well-being. Here is my "Health Maintenance Formula." To make it easier for you to administer, just sprinkle it on top of your cat's food.

The Holistic Cat Health Maintenance Formula

¼ cup brewer's yeast (nutritional yeast)

¼ cup lecithin

¼ cup finely ground flaxseed

5,000 mg calcium citrate with added 2,500 mg magnesium and 1,000 IU vitamin D

3,500 mg phosphorus

5,000 mg acid-free vitamin C powder with bioflavonoids

1,000 mg vitamin B6

2,500 mg spirulina

5,000 mg L-lysine

2,000 mg taurine

2,000 mg bromelain

1,500 mg MSM

6 tablets (crushed) of desiccated liver

½ teaspoon granulated pure garlic

Preparation:

Blend all ingredients together and store in an airtight container in a dark place (like a cabinet) and away from heat. Makes approximately fifty servings of one teaspoon each and should be mixed in wet food once daily. Recommended feeding schedule is as follows:

- 1 teaspoon daily per 10-pound cat
- ½ teaspoon daily for kittens 2½–5 pounds
- ¼ teaspoon for young kittens 1½–2½ pounds

I do not recommend this preparation for kittens that have yet to be weaned (under five weeks of age) because it would be difficult to dose kittens this small. For immune-suppressed cats, you can give a boost to their immune system by administering twice daily.

Oscar's Story—The Power of Support

Oscar, orange, large, and mean, seemed to rule the roost in the feral cat colony located in the woods behind the Chevron gas station. Since Oscar was so mean and seemed to pick fights with the other cats in the colony, we assumed the cat was a male. We, my husband and I, were steadily trapping and neutering the thirty or so occupants of this colony, but Oscar was very trap-savvy and eluded our every attempt to catch him. I started to notice that Oscar was rapidly gaining weight, and two weeks later the realization hit us that Oscar was very pregnant and obviously a female. We set more traps that night and loaded them with sardines packed in oil—no cat is able to resist the very strong smell and taste of sardines. Oscar must have been starving because she walked right into the trap and started eating. The trap closed behind her, and we all rejoiced for we finally had her.

I took her home, and my husband and I released her into the birthing unit that Michael had built for situations like these. If a cat is friendly, we will allow her to give birth in a tiled walk-in closet that we had converted into a birthing room. With a half-door on it, the mama cat can come and go as she pleases. However, when a cat is feral and wants to tear you to shreds, she has to go into the birthing unit. This box is seven feet long, three feet wide, and two feet high with three interconnecting compartments. The mama cat can travel between compartments to a litter box area, a feeding area, and then the birthing area. It had worked very well for us in the past, but Oscar had other plans. She was determined to get out of that box, and after an hour of racing around it, Oscar had us quite worried about her and the unborn babies. She was panting as well as bouncing those babies all over the place.

I asked my husband to leave the room for his own safety and armed myself with a broom. Still wearing my protective gloves from the trapping, I opened the opposite end of the box, and Oscar flew out, disappearing around the back of the unit. I prayed for those babies as I had no idea how she had fit herself back there. I decided to leave her alone and opened the box at both ends so she could come and go as she pleased. She had food and water, and her litter box was topped with some of the mulch and leaves that we took from her colony. This not only gave her familiar smells but also gave her a natural place to do her business until she got used to the litter. Hopefully, she would accommodate us and use it. Oscar, though, continued to growl and hiss at me every time I came into the room to feed or clean up after her, warning me not to come too close. Believe me, I had no desire to get anywhere near her.

After a few days I noticed that she looked old and thin (with the exception of her protruding belly). I wondered how old she was and how many litters she'd had in the past. After four days in captivity, seven beautiful kittens were born behind the birthing unit on a towel that I threw back there for her. We also pulled the unit away from the wall, so she would have plenty of space. There were four orange tabbies, one of which was a female like her mama, two tortis, and one beautiful calico. They seemed fairly healthy from what I could see, but Oscar wouldn't let me anywhere near them. Now the fun began. The broom I used to defend myself was about to get a lot of action as Oscar started charging me whenever I came into the room.

Of course, she was only trying to protect her babies, and we finally came to an understanding. I would put her food in the birthing unit and wait for her to go in to eat, and then I would close the door and take care of her kittens. They unfortunately developed conjunctivitis, so I needed to treat them twice daily with drops after bathing their eyes. This gave me a chance to handle the kittens and socialize them. They were very small and sick and desperately needed nutritional supplementation. I use a kitten formula called Just Born and mix it with goat's milk and a little corn syrup (Karo is a good brand). I also add a little Pet-tinic, which is a liquid supplement containing vitamins and minerals including L-lysine for immune health, and it is available at your local veterinarian's office. I began supplementing the kittens while Oscar ate like a queen. She was given a good quality canned kitten food as a base, and then I mixed in either salmon, sardines, or chicken along with peas, oat bran, and my Health Maintenance Formula supplement.

Oscar had so many babies to feed and was not in the greatest shape herself. She still looked like she had a large belly, and I was worried for her health as her eyes always seemed to be only half open. Once the kittens were three weeks old (and since I was supplementing them anyway), I took Oscar off to the vet. Doc took her in for the day. Because she was so wild, he ended up anesthetizing her in order to examine her. He then did emergency surgery as Oscar had a tumor

Oscar

Oscar's Babies

the size of a grapefruit in her uterus. Doc also spayed her, gave her ear-mite treatment, and vaccinated her for rabies.

We brought Oscar back home that evening, and let her continue to nurse her babies until they were six weeks old. During this time Oscar's health improved until she was ready to be released back into her colony. Her babies, which as a group we called "The Hundred Acre Woods Kittens," were named Winnie, Pooh, Tigger, Christopher, Robin, Kanga, and the runt was Little Roo. They were all adopted and went to very good homes. Oscar was happy to be back where she belonged—home in her colony with her sisters and her previous babies. At least she would no longer continue to populate the colony, and to this day she still rules her roost.

Nutrition played a key role in the health of Oscar and her babies. They all had so much against them that they would not have survived without human intervention and support. What could have happened to Oscar and her babies, if left to survive in the wilderness, can happen everyday in feral cat colonies just like hers. Adult cats and babies die out there everyday. I will elaborate more on feral cat colonies later on.

The Importance of Greens

Another very important component of *The Holistic Cat* diet is greens. Barley, wheat, oat, and alfalfa grasses, peas, green beans, kelp, chlorella, and broccoli are all excellent sources of greens. Phytochemicals, also called phytonutrients, are found in these and other plant foods. Phytochemicals have four major functions in the body. They can act as antioxidants adding protection against free radicals, viruses, bacteria, and a wide range of health problems as well as regulate hormone levels, eliminate toxins, and even protect against unfriendly insects.

Oats are best known for their cholesterol-lowering properties; however, oats also help stabilize blood sugar, ease constipation, control appetite, soothe nerves, and help prevent heart disease, stroke, and cancer. I include oats in my pet's food at least twice a week.

Of all the nutritious vegetables available, I use green peas more frequently than any other. Peas reduce serum cholesterol levels, stabilize blood sugar, reduce the risk of heart disease, help prevent cancer, and improve sleep, mood, and appetite. Peas are also rich in protein and minerals and are the vegetable equivalent of liver without the fat and cholesterol. My cats and dogs go crazy when they hear the seal break on a jar of baby food green peas, and when any of them are ailing, that's the first thing I grab. The chlorophyll, which is the pigment that makes peas green, is twofold when it comes to cancer prevention. It first binds to carcinogenic free radicals and then escorts them out of the body before they can do any harm. I have a thirteen-year-old yellow lab named Jack that's battling heart disease right now, so peas are one of the main staples in his diet. Jack is the biggest "cat-like dog" I know. This is probably due to the fact that Jack was raised with cats and kittens. He loves to clean the babies. Even though he is male, he has always been the nurturer. Because of the high amount of soluble fiber, peas slow digestion and stabilize blood sugar levels,

Jack and Sunshine

making them also a great choice for a diabetic diet. Those of you with diabetic pets should add peas to your feeding regime.

Water, Make Sure It's Pure

There are many factors associated with disease such as diet, heredity, a poor or compromised immune system, and our environment, especially the water. One of the first issues I discuss with my clients is the water supply. It amazes me that people actually drink the tap water here in Florida as we have some of the worst water in the country. Filtration is a must to prevent disease, and it is imperative that you make sure your pets have plenty of clean, fresh water daily. Did you know that a cat will drink from the toilet because he is seeking fresh water? If the water bowl has been sitting for awhile, it will accumulate all kinds of bacteria and other organisms. A toilet is flushed fairly frequently to allow a fresh supply of water into the bowl.

Another interesting fact is that, prior to domestication, cats didn't normally drink water. They evolved in an arid environment and relied on their fluid intake from the bodies of their prey. Back then, a healthy cat would occasionally sip water every couple of weeks.

Tap water is not a good source of water for you or your pet. Most tap water comes from surface reservoirs that are formed by rivers, lakes, streams, or groundwater. The water from these sources goes through a local treatment plant where it is made drinkable for human consumption. Minerals and chemicals, such as sodium salts, soda, ash, phosphates, calcium hydrochloride, activated carbon, and chlorine, are used for purification. In several states, treatment plants add fluoride, a nutrient that many agree is unnecessary. This purification process does not remove the many environmental pollutants that can contaminate our water supply, including animal wastes, pesticides, herbicides, fertilizers, industrial waste, toxic and carcinogenic chemicals, and both human and veterinary pharmaceutical drugs. Over 80 percent of all streams that were tested by environmentalist Theo

Colburn were found to be contaminated with massive amounts of over-the-counter and prescription drugs, especially veterinary drugs. Antibiotics in our water supply are a serious threat and are one of the reasons bacteria are becoming resistant to many of the antibiotics in use today. Over a million people in the United States alone become ill every year from drinking contaminated water. You can just imagine how many animals this must affect.

So just what is clean, pure water, and where can we get it? Well, that is truly a quandary. Public water suppliers should be pressured to switch to a disinfecting process called ozonation, which is highly effective and far safer than chlorination. The reason for such a switch is that if the water has already been contaminated with organic compounds or other carcinogenic pollutants before the chlorination process, then the formation of trihalomethanes (THMs) will occur. THMs are directly linked to rectal and bladder cancers. More research is currently underway on the correlation between chronic disease and tap water. I know of many animals that suffer from chronic bladder, kidney, and urinary tract problems. Also, don't forget that cancer is the number one killer amongst cats.

I strongly suggest a good filtration system for your home for your safety and that of your pets. One of the best systems would be a reverse osmosis system; however, they can be pretty expensive. At the very least, for around thirty dollars from your local hardware store, you can purchase an activated carbon filter for your kitchen sink. The PUR brand filter is pretty good. PUR also sells the showerhead attachment because—keep in mind—your skin is your second lung. Just some of the contaminants found in your tap water include *E. coli,* giardia, barium, fluoride, lead, nitrates, sodium, diquat (herbicide), copper, and radium.

If you think you can pass go because you use bottled water, guess again. Bottled water contains some of the same contaminants. Groundwater is groundwater no matter how you look at it. Recent surveys found a wide range of contaminants in several popular brands of bottled water, including radiation. Consumers are spending hundreds of times more on bottled water than they would for tap water, counting on its quality for health reasons. You are far better off filtering your own water as previously mentioned.

Annually, your water supplier issues a water report that comes with your bill. It would benefit you and your family to read it and make yourself aware of the potential hazards of tap water.

Peanut's Story, Part 1—Giardia

Peanut is very lucky to be alive today. He is a very special cat and to this day has a very special place in our hearts and in our home.

One day, while I was checking on another colony of cats that is located near the one I routinely take care of, I picked up some trash and was depositing it in a nearby dumpster when this four-week-old buff tabby toddled out from under the dumpster to attack my shoelace. I scooped him up and took him home. I had a nursing mother (that we simply called Mama) with two kittens named Lucy and Linus. I figured I would give him to Mama to look after. Mama (a feral dilute torti) wasn't exactly thrilled, but Peanut wore her down, and Mama finally accepted him. All went well for the next six weeks. As soon as all the kittens were old enough, they were given their shots and spayed/neutered so they were then ready for adoption.

All three kittens were adopted their first day out. Lucy and Linus went to a home together, and Peanut was adopted by a vet tech who worked for a local vet. I was thrilled for them but greatly saddened to see them go, especially Peanut.

A few days later I called to check on them and even went to see Lucy and Linus. They were both doing great. They fit right into their new homes perfectly as their young owner loved the companionship and crazy antics of these two fur balls.

However, Peanut's case was a different story. The vet tech had another cat (an older female cat) that hated him. Peanut became very lethargic, wouldn't eat, and soon started suffering from explosive diarrhea. The vet tech took him into work, ran some tests, and discovered Peanut had giardia, a protozoan that is often found in our water supply as I stated earlier. Peanut also had a lot happening as far as immune function, or rather the lack thereof. He was immune suppressed from his recent barrage of vaccines and anesthesia from his neuter surgery, he had been taken away from his surrogate mother and siblings and put into a hostile environment (the female cat), and was now being poked and prodded by his new owner at the vet's office. His poor little body had no chance at warding off the giardia.

A few days later I got a phone call from the vet tech, who was hysterical, stating that Peanut was dying, and she couldn't take the stress anymore, and could I please come and get him and take him to my own vet? He had been severely dehydrated, and she and the others in

Peanut

Mama

the vet office couldn't get him to eat anything. I panicked, dropped what I was doing, and went to pick up Peanut. When I arrived at the vet's office, the red-faced vet tech brought Peanut out to me. It broke my heart to see this sick little guy. He looked nothing like the vibrant, healthy kitten I rescued just a short time ago. I got him out to the car, and he immediately started hollering at me. I mean, this kitten hollered at me all the way to my vet's office. When we got there, he had so much energy and was so happy to see me that I think he forgot that he was supposed to be sick. My vet said to finish out the medication that the vet tech had started him on and give him plenty of fluids.

When I got him home, he ran to Mama, and it was as if Lassie had come home. He was also starving and ate like a champ. I was a sniveling mess. Peanut had obviously not been happy in his new home. Much to his dismay, I kept him separated from the other cats for a few more days to make sure he was over the giardia. As I mentioned at the beginning of this story, Peanut is still with us today. Later I will share Part 2 of Peanut's story.

CHAPTER TWO

Complementary Veterinary Health Care:
The Best of Both Worlds

Conventional versus Holistic Health Care

I am going to begin this chapter a little differently because I want you to fully understand how blessed we all truly are for both conventional and holistic veterinary medicine. There may be times during this chapter when I fully support a holistic approach to medicine; however, a few of my cats and foster kitties would not have survived if it weren't for conventional medicine. It is my passionate belief that there is a place for both conventional and holistic medicine in both human and veterinary care.

As a holistic practitioner and nutritional consultant, I use some of the same nutritional protocols on my pets that I recommend for my human clients. Conventional medicine has its place when it comes to diagnostics and repairing the body; however, it is my opinion that conventional medicine should not be in the business of treating chronic disease. This is where modern medicine falls short—the practice of treating chronic disease by prescribing drugs will only suppress the symptoms of the disease. Therefore, the disease is only maintained and not cured. Holistic health care, on the other hand, looks for the source of the problem and treats the whole body as one—as I explained in the previous chapter.

Complementary medicine is the best of both worlds. It simply means that one complements the other. For example, let's say your cat needs surgery to remove a foreign object from her gut. Vets who practice only conventional medicine would do the surgery and then send her home. Vets who practice holistic medicine alongside conventional medicine, on the other hand, would give supportive therapies to ensure the proper healing of your cat. In this case, your cat would be set up on a dietary regime that includes supplements to speed the healing of the incision and fully support the body.

Homeopathy and acupuncture can also help the healing process. The surgical procedure is complemented by a holistic approach to the recovery process.

Maybe someday in the near future all conventional and holistic practitioners will realize that they can work together in the field of complementary medicine.

To Vaccinate or Not to Vaccinate

This is a very touchy subject and there has been much heated debate between Western and Eastern philosophies concerning vaccines. I will give you the facts from *both* sides of the story and let you decide where you stand in the vaccine quandary. I will disclose my sources of information along the way.

Before we get started, the most important information to understand is how vaccines work. The immune system recognizes vaccine agents as foreign, or as I like to say, foe (enemy). It then destroys these foes, and remembers them (cell memory). When the real deal of the disease comes along, for example the rhinotracheitis virus, the immune system is ready and waiting to respond by neutralizing the virus before it can enter cells and by recognizing and destroying infected cells before they can replicate. That's how the immune system works. I will expand on this explanation in the next section.

I had the opportunity to speak to one of the pharmaceutical representatives at Pfizer, and he stated that there are two types of vaccines. The first is a modified live vaccine (MLV), which means the vaccine contains a virus that has been modified so that it either has lost its disease-causing ability (attenuated), or the vaccine is administered by a route that prevents it from causing illness. The second type is a killed vaccine, which means that the virus is already dead when injected into the animal. Modified live vaccines are considered the most dangerous by many world-renowned immunologists as an MLV has the ability to replicate and then mutate in the body. I was also told by the same representative at Pfizer that multi-cat households that vaccinate with MLVs run the risk of the virus being shed and causing illness in other cats. In fact, we have had several outbreaks of panleukopenia after vaccinating with the ultranasal modified live vaccine. My vet even suggested the vaccines may be at fault and that I should contact Heska, the pharmaceutical company that manufactures them. When an animal is vaccinated, it is exposed to a modified organism. The organism is modified so that the animal can develop immunity without developing the disease—theoretically. By the way, MLVs are banned in several countries.

So, with that said, a killed vaccine should be safer, right? Unfortunately, killed vaccines take longer to stimulate an immune response, and they need preservatives and adjuvants, which are chemicals used to stimulate the immune system response. There has been a lot of controversy concerning the harmful effects of these preservatives and adjuvants.

In the past and present, preservatives like thimerosal have been the subject of debate when used in pediatric vaccines. Thimerosal is a cheap and effective mercury-based preservative used in medicine today. Over twenty years ago many countries banned the use of thimerosal after a Russian study discovered that those exposed to it suffered brain damage. Many concerned U.S. parents and researchers have proposed that there is a link between childhood vaccines and autism, a developmental disorder that affects language skills and social interactions. Even with all the information we have today on the harmful effects of thimerosal, it is still used in the influenza, diphtheria, and tetanus vaccines, blood products, and many over-the-counter drugs. And I am sorry to report that it is also the staple preservative in veterinary vaccines.

A study performed at UC Davis indicates that, in addition to being a direct neurotoxicant (toxic to the brain), thimerosal may also be an immunotoxicant (toxic to the immune system), leaving the immune system vulnerable to microbes and other external influences. If I understand this correctly, this means that the preservative thimerosal is contraindicative to the whole vaccine concept. Why would we suppress immune function at the same time that we are introducing a foreign agent or virus? Well, when I questioned this, I was told that the adjuvant in turn will stimulate the immune system. Some pharmaceutical companies use an aluminum-based adjuvant in veterinary vaccines today. This information doesn't make me feel any better, as aluminum too has been linked to neurological disorders, skeletal disorders, anemia, and even cancer.

I came across an article from *Cancer Research* (Hendrick et al. 1992, abstract) stating that aluminum may be only one contributor of many concerning fibrosarcomas, which are tumors usually found at the injection site. The common site for injections generally used to be on the shoulder, but a tumor in this area couldn't be surgically removed, and the cat would die. Therefore, it is now common practice for a vet to give injections in the hind leg because, if a fibrosarcoma develops, the leg can be amputated to save the cat.

I do not vaccinate against feline leukemia (FeLV) because it is my understanding that most of these sarcomas develop after that vaccine. It makes sense to me that if you introduce cancer-causing agents into the body via the vaccine, the result could be a cancerous tumor or some other form of cancer within the body, especially in a cat with an already suppressed immune system. Do you get the gist of what I'm saying? Many vets introduce FVRCP (feline viral rhinotracheitis, calicivirus, panleukopenia), FeLV, (feline leukemia virus) and the rabies vaccine all at once. With the adjuvants and preservatives, plus all the viruses in the vaccines (some killed and some modified live), how can an animal's immune system possibly handle this load? How can any living being for that matter?

I firmly believe that disease is a result of cumulative effect. Disease just doesn't happen all at once; it slowly manifests over time, which brings me to the issue of recommended annual vaccine schedules. We are subjecting our cats to these vaccines and the barrage of potential health issues that accompany them every year. Do you think their small bodies can tolerate this kind of abuse year after year without breaking down?

With that being said, many veterinary practices, grooming salons, and pet stores require your pet to be vaccinated with most vaccines on an annual basis. Rabies vaccines are now given every three years in most states. By the way, the rabies vaccine is the only vaccine required by law. Your vet will more than likely offer you a one-year vaccine (which needs to be repeated annually), or a three-year vaccine that is repeated every three years. I will explain the history of these two different regimens below.

According to a pharmaceutical representative at Pfizer, animals in a rabies vaccine study group were exposed to the rabies virus one year after they were vaccinated. These animals did not then develop rabies after this exposure, and, therefore, this is called the one-year vaccine. The three-year vaccine means animals in the study were given the rabies vaccine, and, after three years, they were exposed to rabies and showed that they still had ample antibody protection, never developing the disease. I was also told that the one-year and the three-year vaccines are one and the same. The only difference is the study groups linked to each vaccine. And now you know the difference. Are you wondering why not a five- or ten-year vaccine? Well, the next section will answer your query.

As previously mentioned, Dr. Don Hamilton, author of *Homeopathic Care for Cats and Dogs*, states that antibodies from one rabies vaccine are still present in the cat's body for the lifetime of the cat. So, according to Dr. Hamilton, the one-year or three-year rabies vaccine given only once should suffice for the lifetime of your cat, and additional boosters are not necessary.

To further prove this point, I want to share with you the below excerpt from a conventional veterinary textbook that's been around since 1992 called *Small Animal Practice (Current Veterinary Therapy XI)*. The author of this book is Robert W. Kirk, and the editor is John D. Bonagura.

A practice that was started many years ago and lacks scientific validity or verification is annual revaccinations. Almost without exception there is no immunologic requirement for annual revaccination. Immunity to viruses persists for years or for the life of the animal. Successful vaccination to most bacterial pathogens produces an immunologic memory that remains for years, allowing an animal to develop a protective anamnestic (secondary) response when exposed to virulent organisms. … Furthermore, revaccination with most viral vaccines fails to stimulate an anamnestic response as a result of interference by existing antibody. … The practice of annual vaccination in our opinion should be considered of questionable efficacy unless it is used as a mechanism to provide an annual physical examination or is required by law (i.e., certain states require annual revaccination for rabies). (Kirk, 1992)

Interesting? This isn't something these doctors made up; it's how the immune system works in humans and in animals, and all veterinarians are taught this in school. As a matter of fact, if you remember basic biology or maybe took anatomy and physiology in college, then you too know this information. Yet, we continually revaccinate our cats because we're told to do so.

Recently, there has been a lot of controversy reported in the news in relation to the influenza vaccine for humans. The debate is whether the efficacy is up to snuff in yearly revaccination compared to just the initial vaccine. It seems to me that the answer is still up in the air; however, general consensus says that immune response is not greater in repeated vaccinations.

Here is the current vaccine schedule as recommended by UC Davis School of Veterinary Medicine:

AGE OF CAT	VACCINE
6–8 weeks	1st FVRCP
12 weeks	2nd FVRCP, 1st FeLV (feline leukemia vaccine)

if ELISA (enzyme linked immunosorbant assay) test is negative for leukemia

16 weeks   3rd FVRCP, 2nd FeLV, and rabies vaccine

This is *not* the vaccine schedule I follow. TARAA will vaccinate kittens at eight weeks old only if they are in perfect health. The rest is up to the adopters and their veterinarian provided we adopt the kittens out before twelve weeks of age, which occurs the majority of the time. I do not vaccinate kittens or cats that are not healthy. Never let your vet vaccinate your cat if she is ill. It is bad practice to introduce an organism (or actually several organisms in one vaccine, namely FVRCP) to an already immune-suppressed animal. Any good vet knows this. I do not vaccinate my kittens or cats at the time of their surgery for spay/neuter. Vaccines should be given two weeks prior to or after surgeries. Doc also practices this protocol. Nor do I believe in multiple vaccines given at the same time.

One day I got a call from the Humane Society; they had had a litter of six medium-haired, black Persian mix kittens approximately six to seven weeks old. Three of the kittens had died the previous night after being vaccinated not once but twice with the modified live FVRCP vaccine. The Humane Society had started this new protocol that required administering an MLV vaccine through the nose (intranasal), as well as by a subcutaneous (under the skin) injection. These kittens were probably already immune suppressed when they were given these vaccines. When I asked why they would do this to such young kittens, they stated that it was to keep the prevalence of disease at bay in the shelter. These actions had backfired, however, and could have been a serious problem for the Humane Society's other cats in the shelter. They said they were going to euthanize the remaining sick kittens if someone didn't get them out of there. Again this was to keep the prevalence of disease down.

I agreed to take the three kittens—Sampson, Sheeba, and Sinbad—so they were released to my rescue agency, and I immediately took them to my vet. As I feared, they were extremely sick kittens with severe upper respiratory infection. This highly contagious virus could spread like wildfire through a rescue group, so I immediately quarantined them and got them started on a powerful antibiotic called Clavamox, which the vet prescribed (this antibiotic is called Augmentin in human medicine).

It was a very tenacious bug that these kittens were dealing with as they would get better for a few days and then relapse. We finally heard about a new miracle cure for upper respiratory disease in cats that came to us from a shelter in Atlanta. The drug was called azithromycin (brand name Zithromax), which is a human drug prescribed for pneumonia and a few other human ailments. I gave my vet the information, and we jumped right on it. We gave the kittens ⅛ of a tablet for five days and then were to repeat one dose in three days if needed. After this course of treatment, they appeared to have fully recovered, but we kept them in quarantine for another few weeks to make sure they were completely over their upper respiratory infection. They all then went through the adoption process and found terrific homes. Sampson, however, decided to stay with us.

Sampson

The vaccines that were supposed to protect these kittens are the same vaccines that killed three of them and made Sampson, Sheeba, and Sinbad deathly ill. I have personally seen the negative effect of vaccines numerous times in the past several years. I have birthed healthy babies from a healthy mama cat, raised those babies to the best of my ability giving only the best care, and vaccinated them at eight weeks only to have them develop chronic upper respiratory infection (URI), chronic eye infections (which are part of URIs), intestinal problems, or fading or failed kitten syndrome. Fading kitten syndrome is when a kitten suddenly fails to thrive and slowly shuts down. We have been blessed in that we were able to save a few from this disorder. They are usually dead within a couple of days. Nothing had changed in the care of these babies other than their vaccinations. To me, it's obvious that the vaccine created the illness or compromised the immune health of the kitten, allowing disease to enter. I can't tell you how many times I hear stories about vaccine-related illnesses in domestic pets. The vaccine that we used then was the FVRCP modified live vaccine.

I cannot wait for these protocols to change as I truly feel we are making our cats ill with annual vaccines. To take that statement a little further, I feel we are weakening and condemning the entire species. In 2000 the American Association of Feline Practitioners came out with an official statement strongly recommending against annual vaccination in cats. They based this position on research from Cornell University in which kittens that were vaccinated once and tested seven years later still demonstrated evidence of immunity from those vaccines. There is definitely hope and room for improvement in the vaccine quandary. And just out of curiosity, when was the last time you had a measles or polio vaccine? I know it's been thirty-five years for me and I'm still measles and polio free.

Now despite everything we just learned, I'd like to add that I have had cats and kittens come down with rhinotracheitis, which manifests as a severe upper respiratory infection, and calicivirus, also an

Claresse, survivor of calicivirus, with Mr. Moose

upper respiratory disease. These unvaccinated cats and kittens persevered through these two illnesses with supportive care. If the cat was extremely ill, only then did she get antibiotics, whereas, if she had just a mild infection, then supportive care was the therapy of choice. I have also had annually vaccinated cats come down with both of these viruses and some of them had a much harder time recovering from the illnesses. This is purely an observation made on the experience of operating a cat rescue. Panleukopenia, on the other hand, is a death sentence for most kittens and possibly for immune-suppressed adult cats as well. And yes, we even had kittens die from panleukopenia that had been vaccinated.

As I noted before, vaccinating your cat is a tough decision to make. I will say that I do believe that our cats and kittens should have their baseline protection, especially against the panleukopenia virus and the rabies virus. In the rescue, we have had our share of heartache from losing kittens and cats to panleukopenia. Now I wish to share with you the story of five courageous kittens that beat the odds and survived this deadly virus.

The Panleukopenia Survivors' Story

In August of 2006, a local trapper brought a litter of young kittens into the Petco store. The kittens had been tested for feline leukemia and AIDS and had had their first series of shots earlier in the week. It was a typical, busy adoption day at Petco, and we had no available cage space. Against my better judgment, I accepted the kittens and transferred them into a large carrier that would accommodate a litter box.

We usually don't allow trappers to bring us newbies on adoption day. If they have anything brewing as far as disease goes, it could jeopardize the health of the other cats and kittens showing on that day. These three kittens were adorable, but they were very small. One of our foster care volunteers, Lynne Highfill, agreed to take them home and foster them until they were of adoptable age. I put the kittens to be at around six weeks of age.

Lynne called me late that night and said one of the kittens started throwing up and hadn't eaten all day. I told her he probably had a bug and not to worry, but I would check with her in the morning. At 7:00 a.m. the next morning Lynne called me and gave me the devastating news that the kitten had died during the night. She further worried me by saying that the other two were also throwing up. Lynne was also fostering a new mother and four babies for a fellow rescuer who had to leave town. Since it was a Sunday, there wasn't much we could do until the following morning. Lynne said the other two kittens stopped throwing up but wouldn't eat or drink and just continually hung their heads over the water dish. By the next morning the two kittens had died and one of the mama's babies started throwing up. They were in a completely different room in the house, so how could this be?

I immediately called my vet and explained what was going on. I also called the rescuer who was responsible for the mama and her babies. She went right over to Lynne's house to collect mama and babies and took them straight to her vet. She called me with the dreaded news later that day. One of the kittens had died and the others were now throwing up. The vet quarantined them and kept them overnight. They tested positive for the parvo snap test, which is used to detect parvovirus (distemper) in puppies. This confirmed panleukopenia (distemper in cats).

By now I noticed vomit in my kitten nursery and started separating the kittens by litters and caging them to see who was ill. By the end of that week the mama kitty from Lynne's house was euthanized because she was so ill, and all her kittens had died. Two more kittens from Lynne's house died, and I lost seventeen kittens over the next two weeks. I tried everything to save these babies that I'd raised or birthed, and nothing seemed to work. This was the hardest, most devastating thing that my husband and I had ever gone through. Life was just not fair.

Just when I was about to take the last eight kittens to be euthanized, because I couldn't stand to watch anymore die, a few of them actually looked like they were feeling better. I know this was wishful thinking on my part, but my husband agreed, so we took the three that were failing up to the vet and left the other five in their cages. I pushed subcutaneous fluids and gave them miso soup mixed with Pet-tinic (a supplement for debilitated animals, as mentioned earlier). I prayed they would keep it down and they did. I gave them additional fluids and the miso remedy throughout the night.

They were still alive the next morning, so I continued the miso remedy plus a little canine/feline food from Hill's Science Diet and added L-lysine with vitamin C as well. I stopped giving fluids because their hydration was now pretty good. They continued to improve. I knew as soon as they were able to keep solid food down, we were home free. Lucy, Silver Jr. and Smokey (brothers), Malley, and Angie survived this devastating disease and now had lifetime immunity from panleukopenia.

These kittens had not been vaccinated prior to exposure. I had to hang onto them for awhile longer because they could continue to

Silver Jr. and Smokey

Angie

Lucy

shed the disease for up to six weeks, but they were all adopted out to great homes eventually and just in time for the holidays. I had needed a happy ending with all that we had gone through, and after losing twenty-five kittens and two cats, we were truly blessed with these five panleukopenia survivors. I had also lost Wilma, my Bengal cat, during this outbreak because of her weakened immune state. I miss her dearly. Part 2 of this story will be told later on.

Deadly or Debilitating Diseases

I want to take a moment to give you a little more background on the viruses we vaccinate against, beginning with the FVRCP viruses. I obtained the following information on feline diseases from the *Merck Veterinary Manual* as well as the *Cat Owner's Home Veterinary Handbook* by Delbert G. Carlson, DVM, and James M. Giffin, MD. Both of these sources are very useful for further information on conventional veterinary health.

Feline viral rhinotracheitis (FVR)—also called rhinovirus, it is a highly contagious upper respiratory virus (URI) that affects cats of all ages. This virus usually begins with excessive bouts of sneezing followed by watery discharge from the eyes and nose, then fever, and loss of appetite. If the cat or kitten is congested, she may mouth-breathe and develop a cough. Rhinovirus, as it is also called, is a strain of herpes virus and is treatable if you catch it in the beginning stages. This virus is the equivalent of human influenza. Usually, cats can recover from this viral disease with supportive therapies including a cool mist vaporizer, a good supplement, children's nose drops (I use Little Noses brand), and, sometimes if a secondary infection is probable, a prescription antibiotic. Once the cat begins to eat on her own, the worst of the disease is past. We have never lost any cats or kittens to this virus, although some sources say that 50 percent will die.

Calicivirus (FCV)—also considered an upper respiratory disease, calicivirus can exhibit similar symptoms as the rhinovirus but is differentiated by mouth ulcerations or sores (stomatitis). Drooling is also common with calicivirus. Cats can also develop secondary viral pneumonia presenting with shortness of breath. Usually, cats can recover from calicivirus; however, they seem to go in and out of remission. They will have outbreaks of both of these upper respiratory diseases when stressed, which causes the cat's immunity to break down. Both of these viruses are highly contagious. The same supportive therapies are useful in treating this virus.

Panleukopenia—also called feline infectious enteritis and often referred to as distemper, it is the leading cause of death amongst kittens and immune-suppressed cats. This virus is highly contagious as was discovered in the previous story and can survive in the environment for over a year. The mistake we made from the very beginning was that we handled those kittens without washing our hands in between. This disease can be transported on your clothing, shoes, hands, fingernails, and from cleaning instruments, unless you follow proper cleaning protocols. Symptoms are vomiting of frothy yellow bile, loss of appetite, high fever (105 degrees Fahrenheit or higher), crouching in pain, and hanging the head over the water bowl. If the cat drinks, she will vomit immediately. Diarrhea can present as well later in the disease if the cat or kitten lives long enough. A white blood cell count can confirm this disease. Or, as I mentioned earlier, some vets will do a parvo snap test.

Feline infectious peritonitis (FIP)—FIP is a very strange disease and still the most complex and misunderstood disease that kills cats. There are two forms of this fatal disease. The first is called the wet form because of the accumulation of fluid within the body, especially the abdomen. The second is the dry form, which exhibits neurological symptoms, a high fever that doesn't go away, a mild upper respiratory infection with runny eyes or nose, and eventually seizures. FIP is caused by a member of the coronavirus group and is spread from cat to cat; however, in order to develop into FIP, continuous contact over a period of time must occur. So, calling it an infectious disease may be misleading as it isn't entirely true—less than 5 percent of cats develop FIP, which occurs when the virus mutates within the cat. It affects kittens and cats from six months to five years and over eleven years of age. I had to put down a five-month-old buff tabby just recently because it had the dry form of FIP and was having horrible seizures. Charlie didn't make it to six months. Some develop FIP and others don't, and it is unclear why this is so. However, Charlie was always sickly and immune-challenged, so there is no doubt in my mind that immune function has everything to do with whether cats will get FIP or not. Both forms are fatal, and no cats or kittens can survive FIP, so there is no recommended protocol. I had another cat named Mickie that also succumbed to FIP. I knew she was immune compromised, and I almost lost her to pneumonia when she was a kitten. I waited a year to spay her, hoping I could rebuild her immune system to where she would survive anesthesia. Mickie was spayed in March and dead in June. She had developed FIP after surgery. I tried everything I knew to save her, but nothing could change her fate.

Feline leukemia virus (FeLV)—I have known cats to live a long life even though they tested positive for FeLV. We routinely test kittens for leukemia (as well as AIDS) when we take them into TARAA. FeLV is a very difficult disease to deal with because it is highly contagious. It is spread through sharing food and water dishes, grooming each other, and fighting. Young kittens can contract it through their mother's milk. If we know someone who already has a cat with FeLV, then we will ask them to foster the infected kitten until we can place her in a home. However, it is usually recommended to euthanize positive FeLV kittens. We are a no-kill agency (unless an animal is suffering), so instead we try to find these kittens a safe haven in the form of a foster home where there are other FeLV kittens, a permanent home where there are either no cats or one other FeLV cat, or a shelter/sanctuary for FeLV cats and kittens. Supportive therapies are the only treatment for FeLV-infected cats. There is no other treatment. Good diet, supplementation to support the immune system, and a stress-free environment are all vital to the FeLV-infected kitty.

Feline immunodeficiency virus (FIV)—FIV is a retrovirus belonging to the lentivirus group and affects 1–3 percent of the general cat population. It is the equivalent to HIV in humans. Outdoor male cats five to ten years of age are most susceptible. Fighting toms are at high risk for acquiring FIV, and it is not spread by close or casual contact. Cat bites seem to be the mode of infection in cats. Symptoms are fever and swelling of the lymph nodes. An abnormal white blood cell count, diarrhea, skin infections, and anemia can occur. There is no conventional treatment; however, nutritional support is very important in the prognosis of cats afflicted with FIV. You'll see why when you read Tiger's story below.

Tiger's Story—FIV (AIDS)

I would like to take a moment to share a great success story with you. One night, while I was out feeding my colony, I noticed a scary-looking, big orange newcomer that had all the other cats on edge. He was quite impressive. This cat was a long-haired Siberian that weighed about seventeen pounds. He skulked around the woods and intimidated the other cats. We knew we had to trap him to keep peace in the ranks, so we planned it for the next night.

When we arrived, he was waiting for us and was very hungry. We had a carrier and a trap with us and immediately started setting up the trap. Tiger (the perfect name for this cat) snuck up behind us, walked right into the trap, and started eating the food before we could set the trap. And I might add that he was purring all the way in. We laughed, let him finish eating, then got him out of the trap and into the carrier. He was as tame as could be and what a love. So, my guess was that either someone had dumped him, or he was a wanderer. He was not neutered and could have wandered off, getting lost.

We also trapped a cute dark feral torti that was Tiger's pal. We called her Prissy. When we got them home and cleaned them up, we let Tiger and Prissy take up residence on our enclosed sun porch with Silver, who they actually knew as they were from the same colony. They all did very well together.

The next morning we took Tiger and Prissy to our vet to get them tested for FIV (also called feline AIDS) and leukemia, neutered, and vaccinated for rabies. They both looked healthy, so I wasn't concerned. Well, Prissy was negative, but Tiger turned up a full positive for FIV. I was shocked. They recommended euthanizing him, but I refused and asked the doctor how long before Tiger could be retested. He told me that we should wait sixty to ninety days. They then went ahead and neutered Tiger and gave him a rabies vaccine. This was against my wishes as I knew his body was already at war dealing with FIV. Tiger already had a compromised immune system, and what his body was just put through with the surgery and vaccination only made matters worse. Tiger's hair fell out on his upper back and most of his tail, and he was scratching unmercifully. I felt so bad for him as he had had no skin issues while in the colony.

I took him home and started him on an intensive nutritional regime. A fresh raw food diet and mega supplements became a part of his daily regime. I spoke to a friend of mine who is an acupuncture practitioner, and she prescribed some homeopathics to help counteract the rabies vaccine along with a viral immune stimulator. Within one week his hair started growing back and his itching abated. He stole our hearts, and we knew that, regardless of the next test outcome, we would keep him.

Two months later we had him retested, and his test showed a faint positive. I remained very hopeful, and back home we went for another month of support. Well, his next test was completely negative! The vet was very surprised. Since then he's been tested once more and

Tiger

Tiger and Prissy

has remained negative. I give him my immune-boosting formula periodically to ensure he stays FIV free. When you feed your body the way you're supposed to with good, healthy, clean food choices and powerful supplementation, the body in turn will perform and heal as it should. Tiger won the war against FIV. As I mentioned before and will say it again—you are what you eat. I will also mention that Prissy and Silver never tested positive for FIV even though they cohabited with Tiger. FIV is not as contagious as some veterinarians make it out to be.

Now I must clarify that Tiger had what's called acquired FIV, meaning that he got it from fighting or mating with other cats that were FIV-positive. He was not born with it. I have learned that all the protocols in the world can't cure a kitten that was born with it. This was discovered through Iris, a beautiful Russian blue kitty that was surrendered to us because she too tested positive for FIV. The vet called me and asked if I could take her and try my magic cure on her. Otherwise, the owner wanted her put down, so I agreed to take her in. To this day, which is three years later, Iris still tests a faint positive. I knew she was born with it and was not very hopeful that I could turn her around. I must say that Iris is one of the healthiest kitties I've seen even though she is afflicted with FIV. Her immune-building supplements are very important in maintaining her health. Cats with FIV can live just as long as healthy cats if they are cared for properly.

Iris

Spay/Neuter—Mandatory or Not?

As I mentioned previously, I used to have a moral issue with spaying/neutering an animal. I felt animals had every right to have babies if it were meant to be. It wasn't until I started rescuing feral cats and kittens that I realized the overpopulation problem in this country. In Jacksonville alone over twenty-five thousand homeless pets were euthanized at our local shelter this past year. Sixty-three percent of all cats and kittens that were brought in were killed and fifty-six percent of all puppies and dogs. I will tell you now that I fully support a mandatory spay/neuter policy, and I am very passionate about it. I'll never forget the first time I saw pictures of all the euthanized animals, lined up by size from dogs to puppies and cats to kittens, that came out of Animal Care and Control on one afternoon. I was at the Annual Cat Conference in Gainesville, Florida, and could not compose myself for some time after seeing those pictures. I will never be able to erase them from my mind.

Last year I proposed to our city officials that the City of Jacksonville implement a mandatory spay/neuter policy with a five-year cap. This would mean simply that for five years pet owners must be responsible and sterilize their pets. There would be exemptions for serious breeders; however, backyard breeders would have a difficult time getting an exemption. This would also solve another problem of animal cruelty amongst backyard breeders. We had a woman come into Petco a few years back pleading for us to take three adorable bobtail kittens that were rejects from their breeding business. Her husband was going to drown them later that day if she didn't get rid of them. They were considered rejects because their tails were too long for bobtails. We hear stories like this all the time. These are the breeders that have no business being in the breeding business.

The city officials told me that Jacksonville would have moral issues with a mandatory spay/neuter policy and that we would never see it happen here. So, instead we keep killing our pets because of irresponsible or ignorant pet owners. I only suggested a five-year cap to prove the policy would work as it has in several cities in the United States.

This is the part of the rescue business that I hate the most. The solution is simple, but no one is willing to step up to the plate and get it done. Our city officials and animal advocacy groups say the way to end the problem of the overpopulation of unwanted pets is through education and awareness. Well, they have been preaching this for years and our situation has only worsened. I suggested a great mode for awareness and education—I told the city we should put up several billboards with graphic pictures of the piled up dead puppies and kittens after the city humanely killed them. Maybe that would bring awareness to the public, and just maybe it would affect some people the way pictures like those affected me. Needless to say, nobody liked that idea. I know we can't save them all, and that is a cold, hard reality.

My rescue/adoption agency, TARAA, has a thirty-day policy for the new adopter to sign in reference to the spaying/neutering of their new kitty. If the animal is not spayed, then they will have thirty days to make an appointment with our vet. Doc, our vet for our spay/neuter program, recommends that the kittens should be at least four pounds at the time of surgery. We try our best to ensure that our kittens are spayed or neutered prior to five months because a female kitten can get pregnant when she is five months. This is usually when they have their first heat. Kittens grow approximately a pound a month, so a four-pound kitten will be about four months of age. Because we can't hold kittens until they are four months old, we adopt them out when they are at least eight to ten weeks old with a certificate for a pre-paid spay/neuter. This, thus far, has worked well for us. Spaying/neutering your pet is the best solution to ending the overpopulation of unwanted pets.

The Institute for Animal Rights Law (IARL) has a great informative Web site on setting up a mandatory spay/neuter policy. I believe that many cities do not implement a spay/neuter policy because of ignorance on the subject, so I urge you to go to this Web site: www.ISARonline.org/Legislation.html. This is the official Web site for the International Society for Animal Rights. Print out the statute to take or send to your city officials. Maybe if they see that there are already guidelines to follow and laws in place in other cities, then they will be open to implementing a policy such as this in your city. Florida has some of the highest statistics for the amount of animals killed annually in shelters. This has to change.

Preventative Medicine—The Importance of Periodic Well-Checks

The first step in preventing disease is to understand the complexity of the immune system, which I will try to explain in simplified terms. This section will also help you with your decision regarding vaccines and their recommended schedules.

Most annual appointments are set up exclusively for re-vaccination. A lot of people won't take their cats to the vet because they feel that vaccinations will be the end result. I used to think the way around this was to get individual titers, which are blood tests that measure the amount of antibody for a specific virus or bacterium. But according to Will Falconer, DVM, titer tests are not very reliable. This is due to the fact that titers only give us part of the immune picture. Let me explain how this happens.

Antibody is immunoglobulin (plasma proteins whose job is to protect against foreign organisms) produced by B-cells, which are cells made in the bone marrow that are responsible for making antibodies against foreign antigens (organisms). B-cells activate in response to an antigen entering the body and have photographic memories of these antigens. This we refer to as cell memory. In other words, if your cat is exposed to a virus (organism), she will produce antibody enabling the body to recognize and fight this threatening enemy. If your cat then has a second exposure years after her first exposure to this virus, these memory cells immediately turn into plasma cells and secrete antibodies against the recognized virus. This is what happens after one vaccine. The cells remember.

Here are two important things to keep in mind the next time a veterinarian suggests running a titer test:

1. Antibodies are measurable as a "rising titer." However, as I previously stated, a titer test will only give us a small part of the immune picture because there is no reason for the immune system to continue building antibodies for this invader forever. The war is over, so why have a huge army ready to fight invaders that have been defeated and are no longer there?

2. When there is no longer continual exposure to a specific pathogen, the level of antibody will decrease over a period of time. And, unfortunately, the titer test does not measure the memory cells, which lie in wait ready to reactivate and go to war in the event of another exposure. So, when a veterinarian

tells you your cat needs to be revaccinated because of low antibody protection, you'll know better.

I hope this makes sense to you because it really isn't as difficult as it sounds. It is very important for you to understand how the immune system works, so you can make an educated decision concerning the health care of your cat. And while we're on the subject, it is of utmost importance to be your cat's advocate because they cannot speak for themselves. Ask questions, and don't let any vet bully you into doing something that you're uncomfortable with. After all, *they* work for *you*. And remember—the rabies vaccine is the only vaccine required by law, and most veterinarians now do a three-year vaccine.

Periodic well-checks or annual appointments should be just that—checkups. This should be the time when your veterinarian does a complete exam. This examination should include:

- Eyes—for possible cataracts or abnormalities.
- Ears—for parasites such as ear mites or wax buildup (includes ear cleaning).
- Mouth—for dental issues or ulcerations.
- Fur or hair coat check—for parasites such as fleas or ticks. Also, a rough hair coat is a symptom of many illnesses.
- Nails—for yeast or fungus (includes nail trim).
- Heart and lung sounds—for possible abnormalities or fluid.
- Fecal exam—for parasites like hookworm, roundworm, or tapeworm.
- Discussion and recommendation of products pertaining to diet including supplementation or homeopathics (if they carry them).
- Recommendation or necessary diagnostics if there are any medical concerns.

This well-check will cost approximately eighty dollars on average. An annual office visit for re-vaccinations would include:

- FVRCP vaccine
- Rabies vaccine (no licensing fee)
- Fecal exam
- Physical exam
- Biohazard disposal fee

This annual exam will run ninety dollars on average.

The point of this comparison is to show that a veterinary practice can still make money on preventative well-checks as compared to annual re-vaccination visits. It is a no-brainer that many practices today continue to do routine annual vaccinations because it is the bulk of their income, and they fear that their clients would not bring their pets in otherwise. For the future of veterinary health care and their furry patients, the conventional mind-set of medicine has to change. I am happy to say that some veterinary clinics are already offering preventative well-checks and will only re-vaccinate every three years for both rabies and the FVRCP vaccine.

CHAPTER THREE

Your Cat's Habitat— How to Maintain Happiness

Indoors versus Outdoors

It is my opinion that cats need to be both indoor and outdoor. However, I will say that, depending on where you live, it may not be in the best interest of your cat to let him go outside unless you can ensure his safety. In this chapter I will give you safe alternatives and tips for a natural habitat for both the indoor and the outdoor cat.

Cats originally lived in the wild. The exact history of human interaction with cats is still unclear. However, a gravesite dating back to 7500 BC was discovered in 1983 in the Mediterranean nation of Cyprus. The gravesite contained the remains of a human and a young cat. Though this cat appeared to resemble a wild cat instead of the domestic cats of today, the discovery further confirms that cats were domesticated or at least socialized as early as 7500 BC since this cat was determined not native to Cyprus and was obviously brought in.

If it is true that domestic cats have been out of the wild, so to speak, for over 9,500 years, then why are cats happiest when they are outside basking in the sun, or hunting in the woods, or just hanging out in the trees? This is the question many cat owners wonder about. I am constantly asked, "Why does my cat scratch at the door and try to run out when I open it?" The answer is simply that he wants to go outside. Cats know instinctively what they need and how to obtain it. The great outdoors has been instilled in their very being since their creation.

We always had cats growing up. I was about eight years of age when Bodacious was introduced into our household. Bo was a black-and-white domestic short-haired cat. He preferred being outside hunting and bringing us all kinds of live critters. Bo didn't like to kill these critters; he just enjoyed bringing them through the open kitchen window. I still believe his sole mission in life was to scare my mother to death. My mother's screams still echo in my mind. Bo was also put outside on baking days, which was quite often in our home, because he loved to lie on top of the cakes or fresh bread just after they've come out of the oven. Come to find out, that's how we got him in the first place. A friend of my mother's was a baker and worked for a local bakery from her home. Bo was costing her too much money because of his love for warm cakes and bread.

Over the years our cat family grew, and we were forever scooting the cats away from the front door or chasing them through the neighborhood whenever they got out. Mom didn't like them going in and out (that is, as long as they behaved), so we tried to keep them inside for the most part. This had always been my philosophy as well—keep them in to avoid flea issues, diseases from other strays, cat fights, accidents, and annoying the neighbors. That is, until Samantha's kidney failure occurred after being an indoor-only cat for ten years, which you will read about in Chapter Six. After she took ill, I started researching ways that I could give our cats the best of both worlds, allowing them to have the protection of being an indoor cat but also the option of going outside. Here is some of the information that I discovered.

I have read that the average outdoor cat only lives between four and seven years. I guess my cats weren't average cats. Ours lived well into their teens. And today I have a seventeen-year-old named Hope, who you will read about later on, a fifteen-year-old named Samantha, and a ten-year-old named Bruno, who is a feral that found his way to us. They all live predominantly outside. As you will discover later, Samantha would have died at age ten if we hadn't let her follow her instincts to go outside.

Here are some pros and cons for you to consider the next time your inside cat wants out.

Pros in relation to letting your cat or cats outside:

1. *Outdoor litter box*—they can use the world as their litter box.

Bruno out for a morning walk

2. *Live food*—they can eat things like grass, certain medicinal plants, insects, and small animals that they instinctively know will cure whatever ails them.
3. *Naturopathy* (healing powers of nature)—they can get plenty of natural, fresh air, sunshine, and exercise (all are essential for well-being). They can climb, run, jump, and play as they should in a natural habitat.
4. *Yard-guardians*—cats are a great rodent, reptile (especially snakes), and insect deterrent. Where there are cats, you won't

usually find snakes. Unless, of course, they bring them to you. Cats are natural predators to snakes.

5. *Natural protection*—they have the ability to naturally protect against fleas and other parasites. I have to tell you that healthy outside cats do not usually have flea infestation, nor should you have to repeatedly de-worm them. They will roll in the dirt or sand as a natural deterrent to fleas. My outdoor cats have terrific coats and very few flea issues, and I rarely give them conventional flea protection. Instead, I give them brewer's yeast, vitamin C, B-complex, and garlic to help deter parasites. This includes fleas, ticks, mosquitoes, and most worms. Boosting their natural defenses is what will help them most—*not* hitting them with toxic chemicals from conventional parasitic treatments.

Cons in relation to letting your cat or cats outside:

1. *Lost cat*—if they aren't familiar with their surroundings and wander off, they may not be able to find their way home.
2. *Wandering*—wandering into the street can be fatal. There is a good chance they could be killed or injured by a vehicle. Over seven million cats are killed annually by motor vehicles. Cats can also have non-vehicle-related accidents such as falling from a tree after being chased by a dog as in Silver's story (which you will read about at the end of this section).
3. *Poisons*—poisons lie around every corner: in the garage, under cars, in the flowers and shrubs, and on the grass. And even if you have safe-guarded your own property, there's always your neighbor's yard that may contain pesticides and other hazards.
4. *Predators*—a pit bull, chow, or even a little dachshund are known cat killers and are constantly getting out of yards or off leashes to run the neighborhood.
5. *Neighbors*—they may hate cats getting into their garden or garbage or walking all over their vehicles, and they have been

known to trap neighborhood cats and make them disappear.

6. *Fleas and ticks*—if the cat comes inside, it may bring with it unwanted house guests. A flea infestation is certainly no fun.

7. *Higher disease risk*—if your cat is immune suppressed or has not been vaccinated, it may come into contact with other cats that may be ill or carriers of disease. Make sure that all outdoor cats have their initial baseline protection, especially for rabies.

(I'll elaborate on all of these hazards for the outside cat in the following chapters.)

Pros in relation to keeping your cat or cats inside are:

1. *Protection*—they will be protected from all of the above-mentioned outdoor hazards.

2. *Less disease risk*—they won't be subjected to other strays and the possible diseases they carry.

3. *Diet*—you can monitor exactly what they eat (for the most part).

4. *Flea issues*—a flea problem isn't likely to occur, although you or your dog can still bring fleas to your cats.

Cons in relation to keeping your cat or cats inside are:

1. *Escape attempts*—most cats yearn for the great outdoors and will try to run out the door or break through an open window through the screen. Or they will sometimes repeatedly bang their heads on the glass of a window or door trying to get whatever's crawling on the screen or backside of the glass window.

2. *Litter box issues*—if litter boxes aren't cleaned regularly, cats may begin urinating or defecating in areas around the house. It is rare that cats will continually defecate in the same area outside. As insiders, we expect them to keep using the same

area over and over again in the same litter box. I have observed my cats outside, and they will dig and bury their business in a different place each time.

3. *Missing out*—your cat will miss out on what nature has to offer as far as food, sun, fresh air, and a natural habitat for exercise.

4. *Behavioral issues*—most cats may take to marking their territory within the house if another cat appears inside or outside its domain. They will do this by urinating (spraying) and scratching up carpet, furniture, and even you. This is something they would normally do outside, especially male cats. However, most people do not realize that female cats also mark their territory by spraying.

There are valid pros and cons for having an indoor-only cat or an outdoor-only cat. I will now share with you Silver's story and then give you safe alternatives for an indoor/outdoor cat.

Silver's Story—The Broken Limb

Silver was a beautiful long-haired male cat with a lush silver coat. He appeared to be a Maine coon mix and looked a lot like a silver fox. He showed up in my colony one day looking lean and hungry. He was very affectionate to the other cats, and they seemed to like him. I decided to fatten him up and give him time to get used to me before I trapped him. That plan, though, was short lived.

I went to feed the colony one evening, and I noticed that none of the cats were around. They wouldn't even come to my calls. I became worried and started tromping through the woods. I suddenly heard a crash and turned to see Silver limping out of the bushes beneath a tree. With that, two huge dogs came out of nowhere and chased him back up the tree. I screamed and ran toward the dogs. I must have made a lot of noise because they took one look at me and ran like heck in the other direction.

Poor Silver was fifty feet up the tree and had no plans to come back down. I called my husband and told him I was going to be late getting back home because of Silver's predicament. Michael was soon by my side, and together we pondered over how to get Silver back down the tree. I knew he was hurt because he refused to use his front paw.

Finally, an hour later hunger kicked in, and he slowly made his way down the tree. As he came toward us, we noticed that he was limping badly. He wasn't using his front left paw at all. I asked Michael to get a carrier out of the car and to have it open and ready when I scruffed Silver by the neck. I probably had only one chance to get him into the carrier. Sure enough, he was on to us, and I had to grab him and put him into the carrier before he could retreat back up the tree. He was not happy. He hollered all the way back to our home. He needed medical attention and soon.

I was able to get him in to see Doc first thing in the morning. The X-ray revealed that his front paw was in two pieces, and the elbow needed to be pinned in order to hold his paw together while it healed. Doc referred me to a special orthopedic surgeon. I called to schedule a consultation and then immediately cancelled it when they told me it would cost a minimum of 1,500 dollars for the surgery. As a non-profit rescue/adoption organization, the funds just weren't available for a surgery that extensive, or, shall I say, that expensive. I called Doc back and explained Silver's situation. I had heard through the grapevine that he was a very good orthopedic surgeon, although he wasn't performing those kinds of surgeries very often anymore. He called me back and said they would have to order the pin and that he would schedule the surgery for the following week. He did an excellent job, and Silver healed perfectly. Doc also neutered and vaccinated him while he was in surgery for his leg. We thought this was best for Silver to avoid another surgery in the near future. It also solved the problem of having an unaltered male in my household.

For supportive care, I continued the diet he was already on, which is the same diet that all my pets are given, and added in some supplements to help the healing process of his leg. I also had to massage his leg to keep it from getting too stiff, and I had a few acupuncture treatments done on him to aid in his recovery as well. Two months later you would never have known that he even had the injury in the first place.

Silver had top-notch treatment from Doc and his staff. Doc is one of the most caring, gentle, and kind-hearted souls I have had the pleasure of meeting. He has taken the time to educate me on the health care of animals and has donated a lot of his time and heart for our organization. We thank him wholeheartedly.

We kept Silver, and he was a great companion to Tiger and Prissy for a little over a year. I am greatly saddened to say that Silver died suddenly in his sleep the following year. He had a stroke at the young age of two. Doc was fairly certain it was due to cardiomyopathy (heart disease) given his breed of Maine coon. Maine coons are considered high risk for developing this disease.

Silver would not have had this accident if he were an indoor-only cat. And had I not happened along when I did, he may have fared a

Silver in the woods

lot worse from those dogs that were after him. Outdoor cats have to be protected and supervised in a safe area. I will now give you safe alternatives for the indoor/outdoor cat.

Safe Alternatives for the Indoor/Outdoor Cat

As I stated before, we have always had indoor/outdoor cats. I must admit, however, that we usually lived in the country or in a neighborhood at the end of a cul-de-sac. Our cats had to stay indoors the only time we ever lived on a main road. When Michael and I got involved in the rescue business, we knew we needed to create a safe environment for our cats and fosters. By that time our numbers had grown to almost thirteen cats inside our home. We decided to add a cat door that went from our kitchen nook to the backyard. Just outside the door we attached a 20-foot section of the Foster and Smith Kittywalk Tunnel. You can view this kittywalk at www.drsfostersmith. com. This mesh, fully enclosed tunnel went twenty feet out into the backyard and emptied into an enclosed, 6-foot (in diameter) gazebo that Michael had custom built. He used mulch and sand in the bottom of the gazebo, which made for the perfect outdoor litter box. Michael also included several perches and a 6-foot center scratching post. The cats loved it. They stayed out there all day (weather permitting).

This very simple enclosure gave our indoor-only cats the best of both worlds. They were able to get out and enjoy the sunshine and fresh air, they were protected from predators, they could still pounce and catch lizards and insects that were unfortunate enough to get into the tunnel, and I loved the natural outdoor litter box. It really lessened the odor load within the house caused by the multiple litter boxes. We also opened up our sun porch as a protective area for the cats that lived in the backyard. In times of bad weather or if someone or something unfamiliar came into the backyard, the cats had a place to run for cover.

Kittywalk and gazebo

A sun porch can be a great alternative for the indoor-only cat. Wheatgrass and catnip grow very well in pots, and critters always seem to find a way to get into a screened sun porch. Installing a cat door is not difficult and saves you the wear and tear of constantly letting the cat in and out. Cats adapt very well to using a cat door. We begin by taping the door in the full open position for a week or so, then gradually lower the door more and more until the cats master coming and going by themselves. The majority of the cats have no problem figuring out how to get in and out. It's also very simple to add shelving and perches for the cats to climb and jump up onto. Cats instinctively love to be up high. Just make sure you graduate the perches accordingly, so they don't injure themselves trying to jump too far or too high. Also be sure to attach the shelves with the proper hangers, so they don't come crashing down.

Pretty Boy, a bi-eyed (one blue and one gold), white six-year-old domestic-shorthair, and Iris, a beautiful two-and-a-half-year-old Russian blue, are my two FIV-positive kitties. These two were born with FIV, so I keep them separate from the rest of the zoo. They stay in our

Pretty Boy

Iris

master bedroom suite; however, we put a cat door in one of the bedroom windows and designed a screened enclosure for them. It is six feet high and five feet wide with a depth of three and a half feet. It has three perches and wood for them to scratch. They also have access to a kittywalk tunnel, so they can get out into the grass. Eventually, we plan on giving them a gazebo of their own to allow them more outdoor space.

If money isn't an object, you can add the Houdini fence to your property. This fence is specially designed to keep cats in. It usually comes six feet high with an angled turnaround placed on the top of the fence that actually deters the cat from climbing out. Purrfect Fence is a good company for this product and you can visit them at www.purrfectfence.com. Cat Fence-in is also a good source for this type of fencing; visit them at www.catfencein.com. The only potential problem with these types of fences is that other animals, like raccoons or opossums, can get in but won't be able to get out. To get around this, just add a backdoor or trapdoor at the back or side of your property in the event you need to chase a critter out. Most sanctuaries and shelters use this type of fencing and have had no problems.

These are some of the best safe alternatives to get your cat outdoors while ensuring its protection. Your cat will greatly appreciate your giving it the very best of both worlds.

The Three Leading Causes of Death in Cats

SHELTER EUTHANASIA

The leading cause of death for cats in this country is not disease or accidents; it's euthanasia in shelters. It is nearly impossible to get the exact statistic for the number of pets euthanized in our country. However, according to the American Humane Association, almost ten million pets are put to death annually. Here are the facts:

- FACT: Only 2 percent of cats taken into shelters are actually reunited with their owners.
- FACT: Only 24 percent are adopted through the city shelter adoption program.
- FACT: Only 12–15 percent of all pet owners make provisions for their pets in their will in the event of the owners' death.
- FACT: It is estimated that, nationwide, 71 percent of all cats and kittens in shelters are killed. I believe this percentage is very close to accurate because, in Jacksonville alone, 63 percent of all cats and kittens in shelters were euthanized by the city last year at Animal Care and Control.
- FACT: City animal shelters are killing more cats then they are saving—according to the City of Jacksonville's Animal Care and Control, 71 percent are killed, 24 percent are adopted, only 2 percent are reunited with their owners, and the other 3 percent go to research facilities.

The American Humane Association believes that these numbers would change if more pets were properly identified. They offer this valuable advice:

- Be sure your pet wears an identification tag, rabies license, and city license. Include your name, address, phone number, and pet's name.
- Keep licenses current as they help shelters locate pet owners. If you are willing to pay a reward, put it on the tag.
- When moving, put a temporary tag on your pet. Include a phone number of someone who will know how to reach you.
- Don't assume that your indoor pet doesn't need tags. Many strays in shelters are indoor pets that escaped.
- Purchase special cat collars with elastic bands to protect your cat from being caught in trees or on fences.
- In addition to ID tags, consider getting your pet tattooed or microchipped.

Microchipping is something that more and more people are doing for their pets. We, as a rescue/adoption agency, highly recommend it. The chip is actually the size of a grain of rice and has all your identification data on it. The chip is then inserted into the cat between the shoulder blades. Home Again is one of the most well-known companies that does microchipping, and their service is available through most veterinarians. Most vets will charge thirty-five to forty-five dollars for the procedure to insert the chip. There is also a twenty-five-dollar activation fee through Home Again to register your pet with them. Microchipping works and can save your cat's life. Don't make the mistake of thinking that your indoor cat won't need microchipping or some other means of identification. Indoor cats get out all the time, and we hear the same sad story all too often.

My sister Stephanie had a cat show up on her doorstep in a small town called Fair Oakes near Sacramento, California. She and her husband ignored him for awhile, hoping he would go away. When she told me about him, I told her that she should offer him food, especially since he'd been hanging around her neighborhood for over a month. They started feeding him and ended up falling head over heels in love with the little guy. Stephanie's husband Scott started calling him Snowden. He was a beautiful all-white cat.

Stephanie bought Snowden a bed, a carrier, toys, the best food and treats, and he began making himself at home. When she told me she would like to adopt him, I suggested that she take him to the vet to get him checked out. Stephanie made the appointment and off they went to the vet. Snowden was very sweet and was obviously a previously owned cat. The first thing the vet did was check for a microchip. Well, wouldn't you know he found one. They called the owners who were thrilled that he was alive and being well-cared for. They were immediately on their way to collect him. The only problem was that they lived nearly an hour away. They were amazed that he made it all the way to Fair Oakes!

My sister called me, crying and obviously upset, and explained what had happened. She was happy that the cat was being returned to his rightful owner but devastated that she was losing him. Stephanie said her goodbyes, thanked the vet, and then headed for home. She was also baffled as to how Snowden, whose actual name was Squirt, had wandered so far away from home.

Later that night her phone rang, and it was Squirt's owners. They had gotten her name and number from the vet. They wanted to offer her money and personally thank her for finding their cat. The wife explained that, just that very morning, their other cat had died of cancer, and the family was devastated and still upset over the disappearance of Squirt. So it was a prayer answered and perfect timing that Stephanie took Squirt to the vet. He had been missing for nearly two months. During their discussion, the family mentioned that the last time they saw him was on a day when their landscaping company cut their grass. She said he loves the outdoors and at times will go off exploring, so they hadn't immediately noticed him missing. It turned out that one of Stephanie's neighbors uses the same landscaping company, so Squirt must have hitched a ride as he turned up the day the landscapers took care of Stephanie's neighbors' yard too! Squirt was probably stowed away in the truck as it headed south. Thank goodness they microchipped him for, without it, the owners would have lost two cats. If you have a cat that likes to wander and explore the great outdoors, it is worth the investment to have him microchipped.

What would happen to your cat if something happened to you? This is something that many of us don't think about. Make sure you include provisions for your pet in your will in the event something happens to you. Then make sure you let the executor of your will know your wishes verbally. Many of the pets that are left behind today are taken to the local city shelter and will most likely follow in the owner's footsteps shortly thereafter. Please make sure all of your loved ones are taken care of.

We actually got a call from one of the vets we worked with a few years back, asking us if we had room for two twelve-year-old Siamese brothers. Their owner had passed away and had stated in his will that no one in his immediate family would receive their inheritance until a suitable home was found for his two cats (he must have known that his family wouldn't take care of them). Of course, none of the family members would take on the responsibility of the cats, but they did try diligently to find them homes. We were, unfortunately, full at the time and had no space available in our foster care program for adult cats. The two brothers did find a home through this vet, and as it turned out the new owners were to receive five thousand dollars for the cats' care, which should take care of them for the rest of their lives. However, the attorney was not permitted to release that information until a proper home was found. Make sure you take the time to make provisions for your beloved cat. Don't chance leaving it up to family members to take care of.

CANCER

Another leading killer of cats today is cancer. Cats have higher rates of cancer than dogs and most other animals do. Oncologists in the United States today estimate that 33 percent of all cats will die of cancer. That is a terrifying statistic.

What exactly is cancer? Cancer is a disease with many faces. Cancer occurs when cells divide rapidly and uncontrollably. These cells have the ability to infiltrate and destroy healthy tissue and travel throughout the body. Cancer will eventually take over, and the host will die. It shows no mercy or prejudice to anyone or any animal. There are many causes of cancer. Our environment, water, diet, drugs, vaccines, products containing toxic chemicals, genetics, and stress are all documented causes of cancer. As I said before, I believe it is the cumulative effect of all these things that cause the body to break down, allowing cancer an opportune time to inhabit the body. The immune system can only withstand so much. Like a dam that is continually battered over the years, it will eventually begin to wear down and crumble under the pressure of all the forces it has been holding back for so long.

Louis Pasteur said, "the microbe is nothing, the terrain is everything." If the immune system is continually beaten down and weakened, then over time cancer will be the outcome. This is my take on cancer. I have spent a lot of time with breast cancer patients in a support group situation. The entire group of women in the group had all of the following cancer-causing factors in common: The women drank, cooked, and bathed in tap water; consumed an unhealthy diet most of the time; had stressful jobs and/or a stressful home life; were on several medications; and used products on a daily basis that contained toxic chemicals, many of which are known carcinogens. We are doing the same thing to our cats. They drink tap water and eat food products that contain carcinogens and toxic chemicals; we owners use products that contain harmful chemicals like shampoos, flea treatments, and deodorizers, and certain litter products that also contain carcinogens and lung irritants (not to mention, the cleaners we use to clean our homes and the aerosol room fresheners we use to deodorize household smells). All of these factors greatly increase your cat's cancer risk.

It is so important to reduce cancer risk by eliminating many of the cancer-causing factors.

Here are a few guidelines on how to achieve this:

1. Feed your cat a healthy, chemical-free diet.
2. Give only fresh, clean water from a reliable source. As I mentioned before, filtered water is best and the most practical.
3. Use only earth-friendly cleaning and personal care products (shampoos, soaps, moisturizers, etc.). Seventh Generation household cleaning products or PetGuard pet products are both good companies. Stay clear of products containing sodium lauryl sulfate (SLS). SLS is a mutagen. A mutagen has the ability to change the information in genetic material found

in cells and has been used in studies to induce mutations in bacteria. It has been proven to irritate skin, corrode hair follicles (impairing the ability to grow hair—appears, ironically, in most shampoos), enters from skin contact and maintains residual levels in the heart, liver, lungs, and brain, denatures protein, impairs structural formation of young eyes causing permanent damage, damages immune function, and causes inflammation of the skin. SLS contributes to the formation of free radicals, which eventually lead to cancer. Also, be aware of products containing propylene glycol. Propylene glycol (PG) is used as a solvent in acrylics, stains, inks and dyes, and in cellophane and brake fluid. It is used as a preservative in flavored coffees. It is found in pet foods and most personal care products like shampoo, toothpaste, makeup, and moisturizers. Side effects on animals exposed to PG include heart arrhythmia, stunted growth, decreased blood pressure, cancer, and even death. Butylene glycol (BG) is now being used to replace PG in some personal care products, but BG is the only one of the glycols that has not been added to the GRAS (Generally Recognized As Safe) list! Most soft cat treats (not the crunchy type) contain PG, so avoid these types of treats. I will elaborate on the hazards of other chemicals in the next chapter.

4. Limit exposure to harmful medications, including flea treatments, heartworm preventative, and other toxic meds. Instead, try the natural remedies that I recommended previously.

5. Ask questions. Never assume that just because a veterinarian recommends a medication, vaccine, or other treatment, it is going to be safe. Know exactly what the dangers are. You have the final say.

All of these guidelines will help to reduce cancer risk and strengthen the dam so that it can hold its ground against the turbulent waters. Support the immune system as it is truly the only defense against cancer (see Immune-Boosting Formula, Chapter Six).

HEART DISEASE

The third leading cause of death in cats is heart disease, although renal or kidney failure ranks right up there with heart disease. However, I believe that renal failure is the end result of other diseases. I will discuss renal failure in depth in Chapter Six.

I have lost at least two cats from heart disease in the past few years. Their names were Baby and Silver. Both were extremely young when hypertrophic cardiomyopathy took their lives; Baby was four, and Silver was only two. This disease has been reported in cats from one to five years of age.

There are three forms of cardiomyopathy. The first form is called dilated cardiomyopathy (DCM), which has been linked to a taurine deficiency as well as viruses and autoimmune disorders. This disease occurs when the heart muscle loses its tone, becomes limp, and is no longer resilient. The heart chambers overfill and the walls become thin, causing the chambers to enlarge. The cat usually dies in three to four days with sudden onset of this disease. This form of heart disease can affect cats of all ages, and cats with hyperthyroidism are also at risk.

The second form of cardiomyopathy is called hypertrophic cardiomyopathy (HCM). This occurs when the walls of the ventricles become thick and fibrous, causing the heart to weaken and become less elastic. The heart chamber then begins to contract. Cats can develop a mild or moderate form of this disease and live for a long time, or they can have a severe case and develop a clot in the left atrium and die suddenly. The latter is what happened to Baby. By the time we figured out what was wrong with him, it was too late and he died a horrible painful death two days after throwing a blood clot. He had complete back-end paralysis just before he died. I will not hesitate putting a cat down that has been diagnosed with hyper-trophic cardiomyopathy because no animal or human should ever have to die the way Baby did.

I recently discovered that Maine coon cats have a genetic predis-position for hypertrophic cardiomyopathy. Researchers at UC Davis, Ohio State University, and Baylor College found a spontaneous genetic mutation responsible for hypertrophic cardiomyopathy specific to Maine coons. Cats rarely mate with their own breed unless they are being raised by breeders specific to that breed. So, I would venture a safe guess that this genetic mutation could be passed down from a Maine coon to his offspring, regardless of the breed he mated with. Silver was a Maine coon mix. The *Merck Veterinary Manual* says that American shorthairs are also at risk, which would include Baby.

The third form of cardiomyopathy is called restrictive/unclassified cardiomyopathy. This disease is characterized by restricted filling and reduced diastolic volume of one or both ventricles. The causes of this disease are still unknown. Some speculate viral infection or autoim-mune problems.

In 2003 the CDC (Centers for Disease Control and Prevention) investigated the smallpox vaccine in relation to dilated cardiomy-opathy (DCM). Two women aged in their fifties developed DCM three months after receiving the smallpox vaccine. The end report stated that it was unclear as to whether the vaccine caused DCM. According to the World Association for Vaccine Education (WAVE), the offending ingredient that is a known cardiovascular toxicant is glycerin. And somehow glycerin is still used in vaccines today. There are also several other vaccine ingredients (chemicals) that cause severe damage to the cardiovascular system. For further information on vaccines and their potential dangers, please visit www.novaccines. com for a detailed list of all ingredients used in vaccines today. Vaccines are a necessary evil as far as I am concerned. I do believe in baseline immunity, meaning that once a vaccine is given, the body has the chance to identify and build antibodies toward the offending antigen. I truly believe that initial vaccines are enough and that annual vaccines are not necessary. This is my opinion, and I strongly feel that it is the cumulative effect of vaccines that causes immune problems and, invariably, disease.

I truly believe that preventative medicine can change the outcome of the health of cats that have a predisposition to cardiomyopathy. Make sure there is plenty of taurine in their diet and avoid vaccines that contain adjuvants. Instead, use the MLV (modified live) form of vaccines to avoid harmful chemicals and metals that may target vital organs such as the heart. Re-vaccinate only when necessary and based on risk factor of exposure. If there is already a known weakness, do all you can to prevent further damage to the heart.

From Bored to Well-Balanced— The Importance of Keeping Your Cat Active

From boredom stems mischievous behavior, overeating, depression, and eventually disease. Cats that are sedentary and lack physical activity are apt to overeat and gain weight. Obesity is the number one nutritional disease amongst domestic cats. Cats weighing 20 percent over their ideal weight are considered obese. Risk factors associated with obesity are diabetes, heart disease, arthritis, and lower urinary tract disease. The most severe disease linked to obesity is hepatic lipidosis—liver failure. To avoid obesity and related illnesses, a natural safe habitat designed to keep your cat active is essential.

Cats should have plenty of room to run, jump, climb, and pounce. If you're handy, then creating a safe environment for your cat's play should be easy. Most pet stores sell kitty trees and kits that are fairly easy to assemble. Make sure you choose products that are made of good sturdy construction. Carpeted kitty trees are fine as long as there is rope or cardboard included in the construction for cats and kittens to scratch. By purchasing products exclusively made of carpet, we are giving mixed signals to our cats by allowing them to scratch the carpet on the kitty tree but reprimanding them for scratching the carpet on our floors. This causes stress and confusion. You can also construct a series of graduated shelves that are mounted to your wall. However, you must put slip-proof material on the shelves for the cat to grasp onto. Indoor/outdoor carpet glued directly to the shelf surface works well. I have also used the rubber material used for lining drawers or pantry shelving.

Another way to keep your cat from becoming bored and sedentary is to purchase a few "cat DVDs" and have them playing when you are not at home or when you're trying to get something done and your cat is continually underfoot. These DVDs are great and the cats (and dogs) seem to really enjoy them. I have seen several and they are all good. My favorite is the Aquarium DVD. It's a loop of an actual aquarium with fish swimming around. There are also birds, a jungle scene, and mice at play. There are a few companies online that sell these types of DVDs, including www.catdvd.com and www.kittyshow.com.

One of my husband's favorite ways to entertain the cats is with the laser pointer. He runs the cats up the walls, over furniture, under chairs and sends them fishtailing around corners. Just a few minutes a day will keep obesity at bay. They will literally play for hours chasing the silly red dot around the house.

Exercise is very important for your cat as it is for you. So, to kill two birds with one stone (so to speak), you can train your cat to walk on a leash. This will enable him to accompany you on your walks. A harness is a great way to start acclimating your cat to the idea of leash training. When you first put the harness on your cat, he may belly crawl for awhile until he gets used to it. Then attach the leash, and let him lead the way. Never drag your cat as this will turn him completely off to the idea. Most times, if you decide to take the lead, he will follow. Reward him with kitty treats when he does well. Beware of collars that do not break away in the event of becoming hung up. We have heard the story so many times of cats dying because they were hung by their collars. If they get caught up by their harness, they may hang around for awhile but will not strangle themselves.

I mentioned previously that I believe cats need to be both indoor and outdoor. The kittywalk tunnel allows cats to get exercise outside while getting fresh air and natural sun. A good fence system will work well as long as the environment is safe. Remember—your cat was not always domesticated and still loves the thrill of the hunt. Keep plenty of fake, furry mice and catnip toys on hand for him to play with and bring to you. This is his way of showing his affection for you. A cat that brings home the kill is a very happy, loyal cat.

Feral Colonies—The Problem, The Solution

I mentioned in the introduction that one of my missions in life is to help obliterate the massive problem of unwanted homeless pets through spay/neuter and adoptions, and this also applies to the many feral cat colonies nationwide. People often ask me where feral cat colonies come from. A colony is usually started by a lost, abandoned, or feral (born in the wild) cat. The word feral can also refer to a cat that has returned to a wild state after being owned. I have managed a few colonies for the past several years and am amazed at how much controversy has arisen of late concerning ferals. Feral cats rely solely on handouts from humans, garbage, and prey such as rodents, birds, and even insects. We rescued a kitten named Baby that threw up twigs, dirt, and bugs. I was horrified. This poor thing was too young to hunt; however, he survived eating what was available to him. Survival of the fittest is what survival in a colony is all about. The weak die off from predation, starvation, or disease, and the strong prevail to continue proliferation amongst the colony.

A colony usually consists of a queen and an alpha male. This male will chase off other males that try to enter the colony. Cats are extremely social but have a pecking order amongst the ranks. Cats will find other cats no matter where they roam.

We rescued two female kittens from the Chevron gas station. We called these two sisters Angelina and Mickie. There were also two other older kittens there, but they were not cooperative when it came to trapping because they were terrified of people. We called these two kittens, who were also siblings, Sunshine and Rain. About a month and a half later we successfully trapped them as well. When I took them home, I put them into the same kitten room with Angelina and Mickie. They were all ferals and took longer than usual to socialize. Mickie graduated out of the room because she was always sickly but was also very sweet. Angelina and Sunshine bonded together and were never adoptable because of their intense fear of humans. I was the only human they tolerated for awhile, and then Sunshine eventually took to my husband. Rain, on the other hand, socialized very well and went to a great home. Mickie passed away after getting FIP (feline infectious peritonitis) at one year of age. Angelina and Sunshine are still with us today and are still inseparable.

Angelina and Sunshine

The alpha will allow male kittens to stay within the colony until they reach approximately six to nine months of age. Then he will deter them from hanging around. The queen will reproduce and have litter after litter. However, on average, a litter of five will eventually dwindle to one to three survivors. Kittens are vulnerable in the wild. They are threatened and oftentimes killed by predators such as birds of prey, raccoons, foxes, and dogs. They are also susceptible to disease and are continually at the mercy of Mother Nature.

Here are some very important facts about a female cat and reproduction:

- A female kitten usually reaches maturity around five to six months of age.
- The first heat is between five to nine months of age.
- A female cat can have up to five litters per year.
- On average, a heat can last seven days; however, if the cat does not become pregnant, then she can continually go in and out of heat with only a few days in between of non-heat.
- Gestation is usually sixty-three days, and in as little as one to two months after giving birth, mama cat can go into heat again.
- A female cat can have one to eight kittens per litter.
- Early spaying (prior to six months) can decrease the risk of breast cancer in female cats.
- In the United States alone, over fifty thousand puppies and kittens are born per year.
- For every owned pet, there are four homeless pets.

I have read that a female cat and her offspring can produce over four hundred thousand cats during a seven-year period. I have also read that there are tens of millions of ferals in the United States. How can we remedy this problem? I said it before, and I'll say it again and again—mandatory spay/neuter is the only solution.

Mama Cat and Babies

The solution is simple: If every responsible pet owner spayed/ neutered their pet, then we wouldn't have the massive explosion of unwanted pets today. But we all know that there are many irresponsible or ignorant pet owners. They are the same people who allow their pets to run in the street without identification, keep them chained to a tree in one-hundred-degree weather without water, leave them behind when faced with a natural or man-made disaster, or give them up when moving or when the novelty has worn off. We even had someone keep a cat for two years, and then bring it back stating that it wasn't the cat they'd envisioned.

I recently got a call from a woman who moved to a new apartment complex, and after two months the management discovered her twelve-year-old cat. She was given a choice, either the cat went or she would be evicted in thirty days. She, like many people, thought she could sneak the cat in and no one would ever know. This is an unfortunate tragedy and happens way too often. People need to ask if pets are allowed before they make the move. My family moved all over the country as renters with our pets, and we were always able to find accommodations. Most places allow pets, although there may be a steep non-refundable pet fee. How can you raise a cat for twelve years and then give it up? If cat owners were made responsible for their cats' welfare, then stories like this next one wouldn't have to happen.

The Black North Litter Story— The Result of Abandonment

In July of 2006 I got a call from a desperate woman who lived on the north side of Jacksonville, Florida, off Main Street. She said she was taking the trash out when she saw five tiny black kittens trying to forage for food in the garbage at the end of her driveway in front of her house. There was no mama cat in sight. She also said their faces looked kind of messed up or out of proportion. When I asked her where they came from, she told me that people dump them there constantly because she has a five-acre farm with lots of barn cats. I told her to gather them up, take them to Doc's veterinary office, and I would take them from there. About an hour later one of the vet techs called me and said I'd better come up right away because the kittens were in pretty bad shape.

It took all my strength not to fall apart when I peered into the box at their little faces. (I have included pictures of these babies following this story, so you can see exactly how bad they were.) All of them had severe conjunctivitis (eye inflammation), which accompanied the upper respiratory infection they had. The vet tech suggested putting them down even though she knew it was a moot point to even suggest such a thing to me. I immediately took them home with Clavamox (an antibiotic) and eye ointment. I bathed them to get rid of the millions of fleas that were all over them, and I tried washing around their bulging eyes that reminded me of a molly fish, but I was afraid I'd hurt them. They purred the entire time I bathed them. I had an appointment the following day with Doc to assess this litter.

These kittens were too sweet to be ferals, so I figured the woman was right, and they had been abandoned. We have heard of people dumping kittens after they've been weaned because the owners couldn't afford to keep them and didn't know what else to do. The kittens ate like champs and immediately took to a litter box. We keep a 2 x 3-foot pop-up kennel on hand (that reminds me of the tents we used to camp in as kids) just for situations such as this. These little guys were too tiny for a cage as they could crawl through the bars. By looking at their teeth, I estimated that they were about six weeks of age. However, the smallest one weighed only ten ounces. These babies were so malnourished and sick that it broke my heart every time I looked at them. I decided these tiny ones needed names. They were the "B" litter (for the Black North litter), and there were four boys and one girl. Their names were Bandit, Benji, Benny, Bartholomew, and of course little Molly who was so special she needed a special name.

The next day I took the babies up to Doc for evaluation. He knew by the look of these kittens that they were very sick, but their spirit was amazing. They played with his fingers and purred the whole time they were being examined. Then the bad news came. Bandit and Molly would need surgery to remove both eyes as they were beyond saving. The eyes had already ruptured. Benji would lose one eye, and it was debatable whether Doc could save Benny's right eye or not. Bartholomew looked like he would have a full recovery with the medication I had started them on. My question was would they survive this kind of surgery. Doc said he wouldn't attempt it until I fattened Molly and Bandit up to at least two pounds and of course got them over their upper respiratory infection. Even though Bandit's and Molly's eyes couldn't be saved, I had to continue applying the eye ointment in order to keep their eyes moist until their surgery and to keep further infection from going deeper into their eyes.

Within a week they were all bouncing off the walls like most kittens do. Molly and Bandit were initially kept in the tent kennel, but they cried constantly to come out and play with their siblings. I finally gave in, but I left the tent door open with their litter box and food in it so that they could find their way back to the tent when they needed food, water, or the litter box. I have to say that those kittens never missed the litter box, and it was hard to tell that they were blind. When I came in with their wet food, they had no problem finding it. Their favorite thing to do was chase my hand as I ran it along the carpet. Their sense of smell and sound soon became their eyes. They played just as hard as the others and never gave in to their handicap. We soon scheduled their surgeries.

Benji, who weighed in at three and a half pounds, was the first kitten to have his eye removed and sutured shut. He lost a lot of blood during the procedure, and we were afraid he wouldn't pull through. The next morning when I went to visit him at the vet, he was hollering to go home. Molly and Bandit were scheduled for the next day. Even though they barely weighed two pounds, Doc wanted to get them in. He really had his work cut out for him as this was a difficult enough surgery on a full-grown cat, let alone two tiny kittens. The following morning Molly and Bandit went in for their surgery. They both did great, although Molly lost a lot of blood and needed to be closely watched. I insisted on taking them both home that day. I wanted to be there if they needed me during the night. They did just fine and recovered in record time. They were amazing little creatures. All three kittens were back to bouncing off the walls in no time at all.

Two weeks later our rescue was hit with the panleukopenia virus that you read about earlier in the section called Panleukopenia Survivors' Story. I am so saddened to report that we lost both Bandit and Molly during that outbreak because they were so immune suppressed from their surgeries. I couldn't believe that after all they'd been through, they would be taken by this unforgiving virus. The others were spared. Bartholomew had been adopted already, Benji never broke with the virus but was exposed to it, and Benny got sick after the initial outbreak and was left with neurological damage. We still have Benji and Benny today. Benny went on to have two more surgeries to save his right eye and did just fine. Benji and Benny are the sweetest, most appreciative boys in our household. They love to be loved and have a knack for brightening even the darkest days. I will always remember the sweet, courageous, and high-spirited Molly and Bandit.

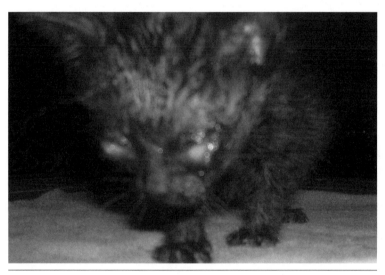

Molly

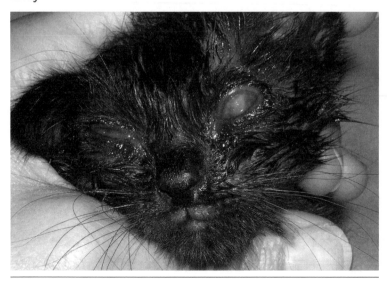

Bandit

Animal abandonment is a crime, and there is a five-hundred-dollar fine plus jail time if violators are convicted in Florida. No amount of money or jail time could ever be enough to compensate what the Black North Litter went through.

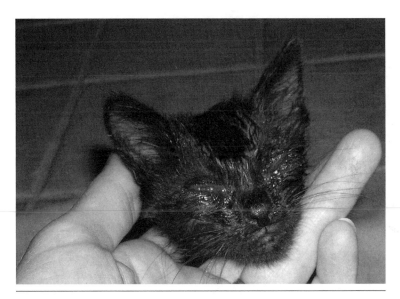

Benny then

Benny now

Benji

CHAPTER FOUR

Safeguarding Your Cat
against Danger

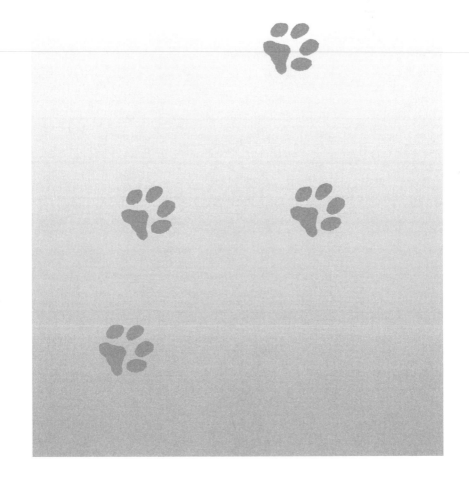

The previous chapter briefly outlined some of the dangers associated with both the indoor and outdoor cat. I will now be more specific in giving you tips on how to avoid potentially deadly situations both inside and outside the home.

Household Hazards

Cats are very much like children in the fact that they rely on us to protect them from danger. Our home should be a safe haven for our furry felines; however, it can be a deadly place for the inquisitive cat. When we adopt a cat to a new family, we like to spend a few minutes educating the adopters about dangerous conditions within the home, especially for the young kitten. Things like strings, small objects such as children's toys (e.g., Barbie shoes and other accessories, GI Joe plastic knives and gadgets), paperclips and pins, ant-bait traps, cleaning supplies, medications, and common household plants can inspire a trip to the emergency room. Recliners and treadmills can also be death to a cat or kitten, especially the treadmills that have pre-programmed workouts. These can crush a kitten in a second. The simple act of getting out of your recliner can crush the neck, tail, or leg of your cat, so exercise caution if you own these types of chairs. Many accidents can be avoided if you know what to look for.

Let's begin by discussing household plants. Cats and plants *do not* go together. Cats will dig in the dirt of potted plants and will more than likely eat the plant sooner or later. Some plants can cause immediate toxicity, and others can be irritating and cause mouth-swelling, staggering, and even collapse. If you suspect that your cat has eaten a toxic plant, you must immediately call your vet and bring the plant in with you. Time is of the essence. The poison control center can be helpful in answering questions and giving advice or you can call the National Animal Poison Control Center at (800) 548-2423.

Here is a list of household plants to avoid:

- Chrysanthemum, weeping fig, creeping fig, and poinsettia—these can cause a contact rash on the skin or mouth.
- Arrowhead vine, Boston ivy, caladium, calla or arum lily, dumb cane, elephant's ear, emerald duke, philodendron, jack-in-the-pulpit, majesty, malanga, marble queen, mother-in-law plant, neththyis, parlor ivy, pothos or devil's lily, peace lily, and red princess—these plants contain oxalic acid and can cause mouth-swelling, staggering, and collapse.
- Amaryllis, asparagus fern, azalea, bird of paradise, creeping charlie, crown of thorns, most ivies, Jerusalem cherry, pot mum, spider mum, umbrella plant, and sprangeri fern—these plants are considered highly toxic and can cause vomiting, tremors, abdominal pain, and complications to the heart, kidneys, and respiratory system.

Another unforeseen danger is the common household cleaning agent. Corrosives and caustics are found in common cleaners such as Drano, Mr. Clean, Ajax, Pine Sol, and similar products. If it contains chemicals (which most cleaners do) and irritates your nose and throat, then chances are it is a danger to you and your cat. Many times people will pour Drano down their sinks and walk away leaving the area open and exposed. Cats love sinks. They lie in them, drink from them, and a few of my cats like to play with the running water. All a cat has to do to have serious problems is step into the sink while it is being treated for a clog. Drano (or similar cleaner) will burn their feet causing them to lick their paws, which in turn will burn their mouths, esophagus, and stomach. Make sure you never leave cleaning supplies unattended. Put them away and stick around for the entire cleaning process to avoid accidents. The same goes for whatever you are cleaning your floor with. Make sure you rinse the floor well to avoid potential toxicity to your cat if she happens to walk on it and then lick her paws. In my household it never fails, every time I clean the floors, I have a helper. Kittens especially love the mop's forward and backward motion. I use a very weak solution of a product called Kennel-Sol. This is safe around pets and destroys almost every germ out there. A diluted Simple Green solution also works well. As I mentioned before, Seventh Generation has an entire line of cleaning products. I have tried most of them, and they do the job. At the end of the book, I will give you a list of highly recommended safe companies to purchase pet-friendly products from.

I now want to share a story about bags. Plastic grocery bags and even paper shopping bags can do serious damage to a cat. Iris, my FIV-positive cat, enjoys playing in paper bags (as most cats do); however, one day I came home from shopping, and I left a plastic bag on the bed not thinking twice about it. I left the room and closed the door. A few minutes later it sounded like there was a demolition crew in my room. When I opened the door, Iris was stuck in the bag with the handle wrapped around her neck and she was flying around the room trying to get away from it. She slammed so hard into the wall that she dislocated her shoulder. By the time she ran out of steam and allowed me to help her, she was in pain and quite stressed. I untangled the bag from her neck and took her right to the vet. The vet told me that cats have killed themselves in the same situation. Don't allow your cats to play with plastic bags.

During the present-opening stage of Christmas morning, the cats all get to play in the wrapping paper (minus any ribbon of course). Last year Michael got me two beautiful wine goblets from Pier 1 Imports. They were beautifully wrapped in a large box and were presented in a Pier 1 Imports gift bag. I threw the gift bag on the pile of wrapping paper, and within minutes Peanut had the twine handle of the bag around his neck and proceeded to fly around the house. By the time we realized what had happened and tried to help, he was beyond stopping. We stood by helplessly until he too ran himself ragged. By the time he settled down, there was nothing left of the bag but the handle around his neck. We were thankful that he didn't injure himself, but it could have been very bad. We learned then that these types of bags are a definite hazard to cats. A plain brown paper bag without handles from your local grocer will give hours of entertainment to your cat and is a safe alternative.

There are a few foods that can really make your cat sick. As stated before, avoid onions at all cost. Some people like to give their older cats baby food because of their teeth or lack thereof. Baby food is already processed and easily digestible; however, some of the meat varieties do contain onions or onion powder, which is a definite no-no for cats. Onions and too much garlic can cause the destruction of red blood cells resulting in anemia and eventually kidney failure. Below is a list of foods to avoid for felines:

- alcoholic beverages
- apples, apricots, grapes (stems, seeds, and leaves)
- avocados
- baking powder and baking soda
- bones from fish, poultry, or other meats
- cherries
- chocolate, coffee, tea, and other caffeine products
- citrus
- eggplant
- elderberry
- liver (in large amounts and non-organic)
- macadamia and other nuts
- milk and other dairy products (cats, in general, are lactose intolerant and cannot digest milk)
- mushrooms
- nutmeg
- onions, onion powder, and large amounts of garlic

- peaches and plums (stems, seeds, and leaves)
- potatoes, tomatoes, spinach, and celery
- rhubarb
- uncooked eggs, fish, or meat of non-organic variety
- salt
- sugar
- tobacco
- yeast dough

A lot of veterinarians recommend not to give table scraps to cats. I sit on the fence with this because I am guilty of giving my cats scraps. They love leftover veggies and meat, and they flip over any fish scraps. These are the same foods that are in the very food they already eat regularly. A few of my cats also like butter and yogurt. I feel the rule of moderation applies here. Organic, lactose-free milk or goat's milk would be acceptable milk replacements for cats. My cats love it when I foster babies because they know they'll get to have the leftover goat's milk.

The last hazard I'd like to discuss is electrical wires. Kittens just can't help themselves when it comes to wires, so it is good practice to tape your wires up to your walls (with masking or painter's tape) and out of the way for cats and kittens to chew. Over the years I have lost quite a few wires to teething kittens, and I am grateful that there were no injuries. Kittens can be seriously injured if they bite into the wrong kind of wire. So it's better to err on the side of caution and get the wires up and out of the way.

In the last chapter I mentioned how hazardous conventional flea treatment can be to some cats. Many experience hair loss at the site of application, and some can even suffer neurological damage. I am extremely cautious when applying flea treatment. We (as a rescue) use Advantage when necessary. Most of the foster families in our organization also use Advantage because it seems to work the best for bad infestations. But accidents do happen.

Pumba and Bobo's Story—Toxic Poisoning

Pumba and Bobo had a rough start to life. They were orphans and had been raised by a family that could no longer keep them. When they were accepted into our foster program, they were immediately adopted by a lovely woman named Ann from Australia. She had relocated to the United States to be near her daughter and grandchildren. The "boy" lived with Ann for a little over a year. Then one day I got a phone call from Ann stating that her mother was dying back in Australia and Ann had to return to care for her. Ann informed us that she would not be taking the cats with her because of quarantine laws, so we agreed to take them back. She was to meet with us the following week and would deliver them to us just prior to departing the country. Ann was very upset having to leave her boys behind.

On the day we were to meet Ann and the cats, she never showed up. Carolyn Fogarty, a dear friend and board member for TARAA, waited an hour for Ann and then called me. I tried calling Ann's daughter's house and got no answer. A few minutes later Carolyn got a call from the police. Ann had been in a serious car accident and was being air-lifted to the nearest hospital. The police had found the original adoption papers with our phone number in the backseat of the car with the cats, who appeared to be in good shape. If they had been in the front seat, they would have died. Carolyn met the police and took custody of the cats. Ann, unfortunately had severe injuries that required surgery, and her recovery would be quite extensive. She was unable to return to Australia for some time.

From there the cats went to the Mercurio household. Tim and Michele were new fosters with the organization and welcomed Pumba and Bobo with open arms. They already had one other foster cat named Mica as well as two dogs and two cats of their own. Pumba and Bobo fit in perfectly with the Mercurios, and there they stayed for several months.

Then one day Michele called me very upset, saying she was on her way to the vet with Pumba and Bobo. She said they were acting very strange, lethargic, and shaky. I asked her what had happened, and she said she didn't know. I asked her if she had given them the Advantage that I had supplied her with a few days earlier. She said yes, but hadn't gotten to it until the night before the cats took ill. I told her that maybe they were having a bad reaction to the Advantage and to call her husband to ask him to check the dosage on the package. She did so and called me right back, saying that she had made a mistake and used Advantix, which is for dogs, *not* cats. The boxes are nearly identical and you could easily confuse the two if you just grabbed the box without paying close attention.

I knew immediately that the boys were in serious trouble due to the lethal effect the chemicals in Advantix have on cats. The vet called poison control and Bayer Pharmaceuticals (the manufacturers of both products) and then administered the recommended antidote immediately. The cats also had to be bathed several times. Bobo did amazingly well, but Pumba had it rough. It took months for their hair to

Pumba and Bobo

grow back, and Pumba wasn't himself for a very long time. The toxic chemical that is so lethal to cats is called permethrin, which is an insecticide that works by paralyzing the nervous system of insects. It is only dangerous if they ingest it. Pumba and Bobo were extremely lucky that Michele acted quickly—as soon as she noticed there was a problem, she made the necessary arrangements to get them help. As I just mentioned, Michele's mistake is one anyone can make because the boxes for both products are very similar. And most flea products are compatible to both dogs and cats.

Never use products that are specifically meant for dogs on cats, and vise versa, unless instructed to do so by a veterinarian. And remember that less is more, especially when dealing with toxic chemicals.

Fatal Flowers

I love receiving flowers in celebration of a special occasion, but I must admit it is rare that I receive them anymore. Most of my family and friends know I run a rescue and have cats and kittens in our household regularly. After one of my cats took ill upon eating a beautiful bouquet that my husband brought home for our anniversary one year, we put the word out—*no more flowers please.*

The holiday season has its hidden dangers for cats, too. We no longer keep poinsettias indoors during the Christmas season because of their toxicity. Cats also like to eat real and fake garland, tinsel, and ornaments with strings. Mistletoe and holly should also be used with caution around cats as the berries can be deadly. Our Maine coon tabby mix named Angel loves to play around in the artificial Christmas tree. Thank goodness he just likes to climb it and enjoy the view.

In addition to a previous list, below are more flowers, plants, shrubs, trees, and bushes that can be hazardous to your cat:

- Delphinium, daffodil, castor bean, Indian turnip, foxglove, skunk cabbage, pokeweed, bittersweet woody, ground cherry,

Angel playing Hide-n-Seek in the Christmas tree

larkspur, Indian tobacco, wisteria, and soapberry—these plants may cause vomiting and diarrhea.

- Rhododendron, horse chestnut, buckeye, rain tree, monkeypod, American yew, peach, cherry, apricot tree, almond (tree), western yew, English ivy, privet, mock orange, wild cherry, Japanese plum, balsam pear, black locust, English yew, and bird of paradise—these plants, bushes, trees, or shrubs are poisonous and will cause vomiting, diarrhea, abdominal cramps, and pain.
- Rhubarb, spinach, sunburned potatoes, lupine, dologeton, buttercup, nightshade, poison hemlock, pigweed, water hemlock, mushrooms, moonseed, mayapple, Dutchman's breeches, angel's trumpet, jasmine, matrimony vine—these plants have various toxic effects.

- Marijuana, morning glory, nutmeg, periwinkle, peyote, locoweed, chinaberry, coriaria, moon weed, jimsonweed, nux vomica, and water hemlock—these plants have dangerous side effects, which include convulsions and hallucinations.

If your cat exhibits any of these symptoms, don't delay in seeking medical attention as you just may save her life.

Bothersome Bugs

Flea bites can drive you crazy. They itch forever once you scratch them for the first time and are similar to mosquito bites. We have had our share of flea issues as a rescue organization. We recently started using Capstar on animals that have bad flea infestations. Even though Capstar is approved and considered safe, you should still use caution when using any flea treatments. These chemicals are considered neurotoxins affecting the nervous system, and there could be serious consequences if used incorrectly.

Fleas are parasites that sustain their life by feeding on the blood of their host. A severe case will result in anemia and even death. I can remember taking in kittens that were so loaded with fleas that, when I bathed them, the water turned red. This is from the massive amount of flea feces, which consist of digested blood. Such kittens are given a supplement called Pet-tinic, which contains iron. I also recommend adding desiccated liver to their food to help re-build iron stores. Fleas thrive in a warm, humid environment. The life cycle of the flea is most active when higher temperatures and humidity occur. They can survive on a cat or dog for up to 115 days; however, when there is no host, they die within one to two days. Fleas mate within forty-eight hours of a blood meal and can lay over two thousand eggs in their lifetime. The offspring hatch in approximately ten days and feed on debris within their area. They then cocoon and go into what's called a pupal stage that can last days or even months. They lie in wait for an innocent passerby and are alerted by vibration or carbon dioxide. When they sense a host nearby, they can awaken instantly and seek out their victim.

So, how do we get rid of the nasty little buggers? You must treat the cat, house, and yard all at the same time. And yes, even if your cat doesn't go outside, the yard and surrounding areas must be treated. Fleas are being brought to your cat from the outside via you, other family members, or other pets that go outside.

Having so many outdoor cats, my husband never uses pesticides or insecticides. Instead, he treats the yard with a natural insect deterrent. The recipe is as follows:

Natural Insect Deterrent Recipe

1 cup baby shampoo
1 cup lemon dish soap
1 cup lemon ammonia
zest of 1 lemon

Preparation:

Mix all ingredients into a 20-gallon hose-end sprayer. Soak down the entire yard, including trees, bushes, and all ground areas. You can also mix one ounce of orange oil with one gallon of water. Mix in a hose-end sprayer and saturate the yard. This concoction kills most insects.

Another option for treating outdoor areas is the use of nematodes, which are microscopic worms also referred to as thread worms. Nematodes control fleas by killing them in the larval and pupal stages, breaking the lifecycle so your pets are less likely to become infested. After purchasing nematodes, simply follow the extracting and diluting instructions that are contained within the package. Nematodes are nontoxic and safe around children and pets. Five million nematodes cover three hundred square feet. Nematodes must be applied when soil temperatures are 55–85 degrees Fahrenheit and must be kept damp. For more information, visit www.gardensalive.com. Most local garden supply stores, and organic garden centers carry nematodes. We have also been successful using diatomaceous earth, which consists of single-celled plants of the sea that are millions of years old. For more information about how to use diatomaceous earth, visit www.blackkatherbs.com.

As far as treating the interior of your home, I use Borax laundry cleaner on flooring and furniture. Use a flour sifter or a large colander with small holes and fill with Borax. Break up any clumps and then sprinkle or shake all over carpets, area rugs, and furniture. Then you rake it into these places to get it down into the treated areas. A broom or leaf rake will both work. Work it in well, then leave it for one to two weeks, the longer the better. *Do not vacuum* the Borax as it must stay down to do any good. The Borax will suffocate the fleas and kill the eggs as well. The hardest part is not vacuuming for two weeks, especially for those homes with multiple pets.

Now to de-flea the cat, my preference is to flea-comb then bathe with a gentle organic shampoo. Burt's Bees baby shampoo is good, and so is Vermont Soap Organics Pet Shampoo. There is also a product by HP Pet Products called pennyroyal shampoo, which is an all-natural shampoo that has been reported to aid in repelling fleas, ticks, flies, and mosquitoes. After shampooing your cat, you must completely towel-dry her then flea-comb her again. This process is highly effective. There are some natural topical flea treatments, although I have not found them to be very effective. They smell really good, but the fleas don't seem to mind. Most of them are herbal and made with lemongrass and a few other herbs.

If you must use conventional flea treatments, use caution and pay attention to your cat to make sure she does not have a bad reaction. It is common for the hair around the application point to fall out; however, it will grow back, and the cat will suffer no ill effects.

Ticks too can cause serious disease in cats. Feline cytauxzoon is a fatal protozoan disease transmitted by ixodid ticks, also called hard body ticks. Cases have been reported all over the southern states from Texas to Florida. Ticks are most numerous in the summer months, so this is when we see the highest incidence. Symptoms of this deadly disease are high fever, anemia, jaundice, and severe dehydration. The affected cat is usually dead within two weeks.

The deer tick is another tick that causes a debilitating disease called Lyme disease. Lyme disease is usually accompanied by a rash that resembles a bull's eye. Symptoms include fever, malaise, and musculoskeletal pain. If detected early enough, it can be treated with antibiotics. The ixodid tick has also been linked to Lyme disease.

Cats rarely have ticks because they are such good groomers. If a tick is found on a cat, it is usually in a hard-to-reach place such as behind the ears, the back of the neck, or between the toes. If your cat goes outside, it is important that you check her regularly for ticks and remove them immediately. To remove a tick, grasp the tick with tweezers, and gently rock it back and forth until it releases. Nail polish brushed over the tick, or a drop of alcohol will cause it to back out of the skin.

Fleas and ticks can kill cats if the infestation or bite is severe enough. Take the time to periodically check your cat to make sure she remains flea/tick free.

Stormy's Story—Against All Odds

One cold stormy night in February 2007, I got a call from a woman who does wildlife rescue. She said her neighbor went out into her backyard to get her dog, who was barking at something, and discovered a very wet, dead, black cat. She yelled to her husband, and he brought out a large garbage bag. When they brought the cat into the garage, they both froze as it let out a loud yowl. They immediately opened the bag and called their neighbor who then called me. I was shocked to see this near-dead cat. When I parted her fur, I could barely see her skin through the millions of fleas. I had never seen such a bad infestation. She was very lethargic and weak. Her gums were pure white, which meant severe anemia, and there was something wrong with her hind end. I took her home and worked diligently to get her body temperature back up to normal and began syringe-feeding her warmed Pedialyte. She was able to keep that down, so I diluted some AD Hill's brand canned cat food and slowly administered that via syringe. I started flea-combing her, and three hours later I had taken hundreds of fleas off her. I packed her in warm blankets and checked on her periodically throughout the night.

At first light I called my vet and got the first appointment of the day. Given the nature of the situation and how the cat was discovered, I decided to call her Stormy. Any other cat would be dead, but Stormy had a very strong will to live. Even though her body was a mess, she had so much life in her eyes. I was very hopeful for her. Doc took one look at Stormy and knew we were in for a long, arduous haul. As I suspected, she needed a blood transfusion to save her life. We determined that she had been hit by a car because her pelvis was fractured. Doc used CP (Couch Potato), a beautiful male tuxedo cat of his, as the blood donor for Stormy. He performed the transfusion, and both cats did great. We also gave Stormy a Capstar pill for treatment of the fleas. Capstar kills all fleas on the host within twelve hours of administering the drug.

I took Stormy home later that day and made her comfortable, fed her by syringe, and put her to bed in a crate next to my bed. At 2:00 a.m. Stormy had a stroke; I was told that this happens sometimes after transfusions. She survived, but she was left with complete right-side paralysis. She could not stand, walk, use the litter box, eat by herself, or even sit up on her own. I took her in to see Doc the next morning, expecting to have to put her down humanely, but Doc said he didn't feel it was her time. He told me to give her another day or two if I was up to the challenge, and then we'd re-evaluate. I agreed because Stormy had already stolen my heart.

Later that day I started physical therapy for Stormy. I supported her head and held my hand under her left front leg, and she pushed herself up and began walking in circles with my support. We did this several times a day for the next few weeks until Stormy was finally strong enough to walk in circles on her own. She adapted to using wee wee pads (disposable housebreaking pads) and did very well urinating and defecating only on them. Stormy still could not eat on her own—we think that some of her senses were still offline. There was no sense of smell, and she only had sight in her left eye.

A few days later Stormy's fur started sloughing off around her back paws. This time I took her to Dr. Stephen Hart, a good friend of mine and a terrific veterinarian at the Hidden Hills Animal Hospital; I really wanted him to meet Stormy and give me his opinion on her condition. He diagnosed her with staph infection and prescribed antibiotics. Her back paws were soon bald from the infection, but after a few days on the medication the sloughing stopped. Dr. Hart agreed that Stormy was a fighter with a strong desire to live.

I continued to feed Stormy every four hours for the next month. I didn't mind, and we both got used to the schedule. Stormy never woke me or put any demands on me. I fed her every four hours as she only weighed four pounds and needed some more weight put on her. She was improving a little more everyday.

Stormy loved kittens. I have a favorite picture of her with a four-week-old kitten lying on top of her. She never meowed but would tweet like a bird when she was happy. Michael and I built a playpen for Stormy and let her roam the master bedroom where she stayed during the day.

One month after I got her, it was time for her follow-up appointment with Doc. She was over the staph infection, and her gums and red blood cell count were looking good. Doc was amazed at how well she could walk (crawl) unassisted. He told me to keep up the good work, and maybe she would at least get to the point where she could eat and use the litter box on her own. I left his office enthusiastic and hopeful.

Stormy's favorite time of the day was when I took her outside in the sun to the warm concrete of the driveway. She would walk back and forth down the driveway and visit the other cats in the yard. When she tired, I brought her back in. Then one stormy night in July, Stormy had a grand mal seizure and died within three minutes. My heart was shattered. I couldn't believe she was gone. After all she'd endured, it just wasn't fair. I was a mess for weeks after she died. I had a daily ritual with her and planned my life around her needs only to have her taken from me. I was lost and greatly saddened.

I soon realized that my job with Stormy had been to give her a soft place to land and a little more time on earth. I was chosen to be her temporary guardian. These moments had been about her, not me. She was only mine to have for a very short time. While she was with us, Stormy received unconditional love and care. The time I had with her was a blessing. Stormy taught me patience and the true meaning of strength, hope, and perseverance. She was here to teach me—not the other way around. I have learned so much from many of these angels, and that is why I have chosen to do rescue.

Stormy truly beat the odds. She had so much against her, and technically shouldn't have survived that cold, stormy night. She might have survived the injury from her accident, but without intervention she would have died within a few days from the fleas that were draining her blood.

Don't let your cat become ill from these parasites. Protect her with periodic flea treatment. Every now and then run a flea comb down her back to check for fleas and treat her accordingly.

Wandering Wildlife

For many outdoor cats wildlife attacks pose a formidable threat. Depending on where you live, there are many species of wildlife and domestic animals that can kill or seriously injure cats. Wolves, foxes, bears, dogs, large cats, alligators, birds of prey, rattlesnakes or water moccasins, and even hungry or sick raccoons are all adversaries to cats. Raccoons in general will not antagonize a cat; they actually cohabit within colonies quite well.

A raccoon we named Henny once lived on our property. Henny would eat with the cats every night and even share their bowls at times. She was extremely tame and would sometimes bring her babies around and other raccoon friends, too. We have never had an incidence with a raccoon attack on our cats; however, a sick, disoriented raccoon can be a threat to cats. TARAA has taken in many sick raccoons; however, they must be caged and kept separately from the other foster animals in our care. A sick raccoon always carries the threat of rabies, so extreme caution is exercised. I usually try to get them to a local wildlife rehab center where there are professionals that know how to handle them.

One day I heard a cat fight break out in the backyard and ran outside to break it up. It turned out that it wasn't a cat fight, but a young raccoon was menacing one of my cats named Tessa. He was wobbling all over the place and following her all over the yard. Tessa wasn't being confrontational; she was just trying to get away from him. As I got closer, I saw the dazed look in his eyes and knew he was sick. I got a large carrier and coaxed him into it. He died three hours later from distemper. Distemper is almost always a death sentence for a raccoon. Earlier I mentioned Dr. Hart, and I must say that TARAA is very thankful to him for the work he does with wildlife. He is one of the few wildlife veterinarians in Jacksonville and the only one I know of that will help raccoons. Please use extreme caution when dealing with wildlife. Wild animals are unpredictable and can cause serious injury to you and your pets. Call the authorities and let the professionals handle the situation at hand.

I guess I should also include humans in the category of a threat to cats. A few years back we had a feral cat problem on the north side of Jacksonville. Word got out and some men, who I will call "undesirables" (you can fill in your own word), took it upon themselves to

Henny

Henny with Tiger and Will

handle the problem. Armed with several shotguns and a few cases of beer, these undesirables slaughtered twenty-five cats and kittens before anyone could do anything about it. Another issue has been the poisoning of feral cats. As a rescue we had several complaints of businesses threatening to poison the cats that would not leave their premises. Some actually came through on their threats and were later fined for animal cruelty. People never cease to amaze me. My husband says that the more he deals with cats, the less he likes humans.

Living in northern Florida, we have quite a few animals to contend with in the wild. Jaguars, bobcats, black bears, alligators, owls, hawks, eagles, snakes, and wild dogs and hogs are all predators to cats and kittens. Kittens born in the wild are especially vulnerable to predators. Numerous people have called us, pleading, to come trap baby kittens in their yard because the hawks and owls were carrying them off, and they couldn't bear to watch or hear anymore of them die. Hawks hunt by day and owls by night.

I used to live near a large lake in a nice neighborhood here in Florida, and we often heard of small animals (mostly dogs and cats) disappearing while drinking or playing near the lake. Michael and I had to wade into this lake once in order to rescue a duck that had a huge chunk eaten out of its side. We suspected an alligator snapping turtle had done the work. When we investigated, however, we discovered that there was a 4-foot gator in the lake. We are thankful that we were bigger than it was. Gators can be quite aggressive. The authorities (Wildlife Game and Commission) won't remove a gator unless it is a full four feet in length. This one was close enough, so they trapped it and escorted it to a less populated area. Snakes, on the other hand, are usually afraid of cats and will retreat whenever cats are present; however, some cats are not very smart and will antagonize a full-grown rattler or moccasin. As a result, they will suffer a venomous bite. I recently found out that most veterinarians do not carry anti-venom as it is expensive and not widely used. If you live in an area where snakes are a problem, then I would advise you to call the veterinary clinics in your area to see who carries anti-venom. It could save your pet's life.

Recently, a woman came into Petco looking for an orange and white tabby kitten. When we interviewed her as a potential adoptee, she told us a horrifying story. She told us that one day while she was gardening, her cat of twelve years was in the driveway basking in the sun when she heard him in distress and ran to his rescue. By the time she got to him, he was already in the jaws of two large ferocious pit bull dogs, also called American pit bull terriers. These dogs were playing tug-of-war with her cat. She ran and got the hose, but, by the time she scared them off, the cat was already dead. She was devastated. She'd never seen the dogs in her neighborhood; however, they both wore collars, so they must have come from one of the surrounding neighborhoods. That poor woman was bawling while telling the story to us. She had raised this cat since he was three weeks old.

This story and so many others like it are real tragedies. Irresponsible pet owners are oftentimes the culprits when it comes to dog attacks on both animals and humans. Dogs should not be permitted to roam streets and neighborhoods. This cat attack could easily have been a small child attack. I have personally watched my neighbors open their doors and let their pit bulls run loose. I have also called the authorities many times complaining about this. I was told that until those dogs leave the owners' property, there was nothing the authorities could do. This is unfortunate for any innocent passersby, whether human or animal. It is my personal opinion that owners of aggressive-breed dogs should have to have fenced yards in order to have these animals as pets.

These are all reasons that we must protect and contain our cats within the yard. Do not let them roam freely. Leash-train your cat if you do not have a fenced-in yard or have an enclosure built for her. It only takes a second for an accident or attack to happen.

Medication Madness

I want to elaborate on the many dangers associated with various medications, both human and veterinary. Cats, like some humans, are very sensitive when it comes to medications. The most common side effects are lethargy, depression, diarrhea, constipation, upset stomach, loss or increase of appetite, vomiting, anxiety, and even aggression. Many medications can even cause seizures in some animals. It is very important to ask your vet about possible side effects when a medication is prescribed for your cat. Don't take it for granted that prescription medications aren't dangerous. Many human drugs are the same ones used in veterinary medicine. And keep in mind that most drugs are first tested on animals, then humans. Here are a few examples of frequently prescribed medications and their side effects per the *Springhouse Nurse's Drug Guide 2005*. Please note that italicized side effects mean they were the most commonly experienced by people in that particular drug's clinical trial.

Prednisone (pred' ni sone)—(steroid)

ADVERSE SIDE EFFECTS

- CNS [central nervous system]: *Vertigo, headache,* paresthesias, insomnia, convulsions, psychosis, cataracts, increased intraocular pressure, glaucoma (long-term therapy)
- CV [cardiovascular]: Hypotension, shock, hypertension and CHF secondary to fluid retention, thromboembolism, thrombophlebitis, fat embolism, cardiac arrhythmias
- Electrolyte imbalance: *Na+ and fluid retention,* hypokalemia, hypocalcemia
- Endocrine: Amenorrhea, irregular menses, growth retardation, decreased carbohydrate tolerance, diabetes mellitus, cushingoid state (long-term effect), increased blood sugar, increased serum cholesterol, decreased T_3 and T_4 levels, HPA suppression with systemic therapy longer than 5 days
- GI [gastrointestinal]: Peptic or esophageal ulcer, pancreatitis, abdominal distention, nausea, vomiting, *increased appetite, weight gain* (long-term therapy)
- Hypersensitivity: Hypersensitivity or anaphylactoid reactions
- Musculoskeletal: Muscle weakness, steroid myopathy, loss of muscle mass, osteoporosis, spontaneous fractures (long-term therapy)

Other: *Immunosuppression, aggravation or masking of infections; impaired wound healing;* thin, fragile skin; petechiae, ecchymoses, purpura, striae; subcutaneous fat atrophy

Dexamethasone (dex a meth' a sone)—(steroid)

ADVERSE EFFECTS

Adverse effects depend on dose, route, and duration of therapy. The first list is primarily associated with absorption; the list following is related to specific routes of administration.

- CNS: Convulsions, *vertigo, headaches,* pseudotumor cerebri, *euphoria, insomnia, mood swings, depression,* psychosis, intracerebral hemorrhage, reversible cerebral atrophy in infants, cataracts, increased intraocular pressure, glaucoma
- CV: *Hypertension,* CHF, necrotizing angiitis
- Endocrine: Growth retardation, decreased carbohydrate tolerance, diabetes mellitus, cushingoid state, *secondary adrenocortical and pituitary unresponsiveness*
- GI: Peptic or esophageal ulcer, pancreatitis, abdominal distention
- GU [genitourinary]: *Amenorrhea, irregular menses*
- Hematologic: *Fluid and electrolyte disturbances,* negative nitrogen balance, increased blood sugar, glycosuria, increased serum cholesterol, decreased serum T_3 and T_4 levels
- Hypersensitivity: Anaphylactoid or hypersensitivity reactions
- Musculoskeletal: *Muscle weakness,* steroid myopathy, loss of muscle mass, osteoporosis, spontaneous fractures
- Other: *Impaired wound healing; petechiae; ecchymoses; increased sweating; thin and fragile skin; acne; immunosuppression and masking of signs of infection;* activation of latent infections, including tuberculosis, fungal, and viral eye infections; pneumonia; abscess; septic infection; GI and GU infections

INTRA-ARTICULAR

- Musculoskeletal: Osteonecrosis, tendon rupture, infection

INTRALESIONAL THERAPY

- CNS: Blindness (when used on face and head—rare)

RESPIRATORY INHALANT

- Endocrine: Suppression of HPA function due to systemic absorption
- Respiratory: Oral, laryngeal, pharyngeal irritation
- Other: Fungal infections

INTRANASAL

- CNS: Headache
- Dermatologic: Urticaria
- Endocrine: Suppression of HPA function due to systemic absorption
- GI: Nausea
- Respiratory: Nasal irritation, fungal infections, epistaxis, rebound congestion, perforation of the nasal septum, anosmia

TOPICAL DERMATOLOGIC OINTMENTS, CREAMS, SPRAYS

- Endocrine: Suppression of HPA function due to systemic absorption, growth retardation in children (children may be at special risk for systemic absorption because of their large skin surface area to body weight ratio)
- Local: Local burning, irritation, acneiform lesions, striae, skin atrophy

OPHTHALMIC PREPARATIONS

- Endocrine: Suppression of HPA function due to systemic absorption; more common with long-term use
- Local: Infections, especially fungal; glaucoma, cataracts with long-term use

(*Springhouse Nurse's Drug Guide 2005*, 2004)

Long-term use of steroids can lead to diabetes in humans as well as in animals. Any pharmaceutical company will tell you that medications are to be used as therapy until the underlying problem is solved and corrected, and then the medication should be either weaned off or stopped altogether. Very few medications were designed to be taken indefinitely or chronically. Steroids should also *never* be used when an infection is suspected and especially *never* to try to reduce a fever. Some veterinarians use dexamethasone to reduce high fevers, but this action only worsens the condition of the cat. Administering dexamethasone when there is a raging infection can be fatal. Steroids cause immunosuppression and can mask the signs of a serious infection. I will share an example later on in Kiera's story.

Antibiotics can cause a lot of GI (gastrointestinal) issues in animals, especially cats. They also cause immunosuppression. I think of antibiotics as mini-chemotherapy—they destroy both red and white blood cells, just like chemotherapy, ideally killing the bacteria as well. This is why it is highly recommended *not* to use antibiotics for an infection that is of viral origin. The Centers for Disease Control (CDC) states that antibiotics should not be considered therapy for viral infections because viruses do not respond to antibiotics and at times may worsen the condition. For more information, visit www.cdc.gov/drugresistance.

Only use antibiotics when absolutely necessary, and don't forget that symptoms like a runny or stuffed nose, watery eyes, or a fever are the body's way of fighting off offending organisms. Most illnesses in cats are viral, not bacterial. Here are a few of the most commonly prescribed antibiotics.

Amoxicillin trihydrate (a mox i sill' in)—(antibiotic)

ADVERSE SIDE-EFFECTS

- CNS: Lethargy, hallucinations, seizures
- GI: *Glossitis, stomatitis, gastritis, sore mouth,* furry tongue, black "hairy" tongue, *nausea, vomiting, diarrhea, abdominal pain,* bloody diarrhea, enterocolitis, pseudomembranous colitis, nonspecific hepatitis

- GU: Nephritis
- Hematologic: Anemia, thrombocytopenia, leukopenia, neutropenia, prolonged bleeding time
- Hypersensitivity: *Rash, fever, wheezing,* anaphylaxis
- Other: *Superinfections*—oral and rectal moniliasis, vaginitis

Gentamicin sulfate (jen ta mye' sin)—(antibiotic)

ADVERSE SIDE-EFFECTS

- CNS: Ototoxicity—*tinnitus, dizziness,* vertigo, deafness (partially reversible to irreversible), vestibular paralysis, confusion, disorientation, depression, lethargy, nystagmus, visual disturbances, headache, *numbness, tingling,* tremor, paresthesias, muscle twitching, convulsions, muscular weakness, neuromuscular blockade
- CV: Palpitations, hypotension, hypertension
- GI: Hepatic toxicity, *nausea, vomiting, anorexia,* weight loss, stomatitis, increased salivation
- GU: Nephrotoxicity
- Hematologic: *Leukemoid reaction,* agranulocytosis, granulocytosis, leukopenia, leukocytosis, thrombocytopenia, eosinophilia, pancytopenia, anemia, hemolytic anemia, increased or decreased reticulocyte count, electrolyte disturbances
- Hypersensitivity: *Purpura, rash,* urticaria, exfoliative dermatitis, itching
- Local: *Pain, irritation, arachnoiditis at IM injection sites*
- Other: Fever, apnea, splenomegaly, joint pain, *superinfections*

OPHTHALMIC PREPARATIONS

- Local: *Transient irritation, burning, stinging, itching,* angioneurotic edema, urticaria, vesicular and maculopapular dermatitis

TOPICAL DERMATOLOGIC PREPARATIONS

- Local: *Photosensitization,* superinfections

Levofloxacin (lee voe flox' a sin), Levaquin—(antibiotic)

ADVERSE SIDE-EFFECTS

- CNS: *Headache*, dizziness, *insomnia*, fatigue, somnolence, blurred vision
- GI: *Nausea*, vomiting, dry mouth, *diarrhea*, abdominal pain (occur less with this drug than with oflaxacin), constipation, flatulence
- Hematologic: Elevated BUN, AST, ALT, serum creatinine, and alkaline phosphatase; neutropenia, anemia
- Other: Fever, rash, photosensitivity, *muscle and joint tenderness*

(*Springhouse Nurse's Drug Guide 2005*, 2004)

Many of us are guilty of running to the vet as soon as our cat starts sneezing or sniffling. However, give your cats a chance to work it out on their own before intervening. A fever can be brought down by placing a cool water bottle or a freezer pack under their bedding. If the cat keeps getting off the cool area, then confine her to a pet carrier, limiting her space. A stuffy nose can get immediate relief with Little Noses decongestant saline nose spray/drops. We use this treatment anytime upper respiratory infection hits our rescue. Another remedy we use is called Similasan eye drops. The regular or the allergy formula is great for treating conjunctivitis or irritated eyes. It is a natural homeopathic formula specific to eye problems. Your local drugstore should carry it.

The last medication I'd like to discuss is one of the most prescribed in veterinary medicine—Synthroid. This drug is usually prescribed for hypothyroidism.

Levothyroxine sodium (L-thyroxine, T_4) (lee voe thye rox' een) Synthroid (thyroid hormone)

ADVERSE SIDE-EFFECTS

- CNS: Tremors, headache, nervousness, insomnia
- CV: Palpitations, tachycardia, angina, cardiac arrest

- Dermatologic: Allergic skin reactions, partial loss of hair in first few months of therapy in children
- GI: Diarrhea, nausea, vomiting

(*Springhouse Nurse's Drug Guide 2005*, 2004)

You have to pay special attention to your cat during the first week of Synthroid therapy. Notify your vet if nervousness, tremors, or sleeplessness occurs. You may need to have the prescription adjusted to a smaller dose for your cat. I am not convinced that Synthroid doesn't cause heart problems, and I believe that such long-term therapy can predispose your cat to such issues as it does in humans. A holistic vet will give you alternative options to Synthroid. I have been very successful using homeopathics for hypothyroidism.

No matter what medication your cat is prescribed, *always* use caution when administering the drug. Watch for side effects and notify your vet immediately if a problem should arise. Remember your cat cannot speak for herself; therefore, you must be her advocate.

Kiera's Story—Deadly Medication

Kiera is a beautiful torbi, which means she is a tortoiseshell and tabby mix. She was brought to me by a trapper a few years back as I have a reputation of taking in unwanted, pregnant cats. Another rescue group actually called my operation "the underground maternity ward for strays." As I have noted many times before, we are a no-kill organization, so aborting unborn kittens goes against our beliefs. Others don't share our views.

I was only hesitant in taking Kiera because the "maternity ward" was more than full already. Chloe, a jet black feral mama had already delivered four babies on the sun porch in the birthing unit. She had two boys and two girls. Vana, a chocolate point Persian/Siamese mix; Gray Belle, a gray psychotic tabby; and LeAnne, an orange tabby, were already taking up residence in the maternity room. This was a large, extra bedroom where we converted the walk-in closet into a 3 x 4-foot birthing area with a half door on it so mama could come and go. The babies would be contained and protected within this closet. The rest of the room was divided in two with a mama-to-be on each side. The only space left in my home was a small 6 x 9-foot area of my master bedroom suite that was being used as an office. We cleared this room and set it up for Kiera. Did I also mention that all four mama cats were due within a week of each other? Five mama cats and who knows how many kittens would be the end result. This was to be a most memorable year for cat rescue in our household.

LeAnne had her babies first with no problems. She delivered at around 3:00 a.m., and, when I awoke the next morning, she had had five beautiful babies. Two were calico, and the other three were orange tabby boys.

Two days later I wasn't feeling well, so I cancelled my appointments for the day and went back to bed. It is very fortunate that I didn't go to work as I suddenly heard a cat in distress. I ran into the birthing room and saw that Vana was having difficulty. She was tiring rapidly and couldn't deliver the first baby. I panicked and took her up to the animal hospital to see Doc. He observed her and helped her deliver a huge long-haired black-and-white boy that we named Vachel, which means a small cow in French. After that the next three babies were uneventful. In addition to Vachel, she had two long-haired gray boys and one long-haired black girl.

I took her and the four babies back home to discover that Gray Belle had birthed her first baby. I knew something was wrong because she wouldn't tend to it. I opened the sac around the kitten and placed the kitten on Gray Belle. She stood up and tried to drag the baby behind the birthing box by the head. I took the baby away from her and called the vet for some advice. He said that she probably instinctively knew that there was something wrong with the babies and would rather kill the babies herself then let them suffer and die a horrible death. I was horrified! The other option was that she was just a bad or inexperienced mother. I took the first kitten in to Vana and prayed that she would take her. Vana immediately started cleaning her, and I ran back inside to help Gray Belle's other unborn babies.

Over the next three hours Gray Belle had five more kittens and wanted nothing to do with them. Vana's babies were fed and sleeping soundly, so I slipped Gray Belle's remaining kittens in to Vana, and she wholeheartedly accepted them all. LeAnne (the orange mama cat) wouldn't take any of Gray Belle's kittens. And if the feral cat Chloe rejected them, I would have a hard time getting them out of her birthing unit once I dropped them in to her, so Vana was my only chance. However, I knew I couldn't saddle Vana with eleven babies. I also needed to know if Gray Belle was a bad mother or just knew that her babies had health problems. After all, they were half the size of Vana's babies.

After much deliberation I decided to do a swap. I took Vana's babies in to Gray Belle and she took to them right away. She cleaned them and let them nurse. I was thrilled that Gray Belle wasn't a bad mama, but I kept a close watch on her over the next few hours. Vana seemed perfectly content with her six new babies. I was nervous about the state of their health, though, and sure enough, over the next month, three of them died of failed kitten syndrome. The three remaining were still tiny, but Vana never gave up on them. I still have one of the kittens today, and her name is Darla, a sweet gray tabby with white paws and chest (also called a tabby tuxedo).

Kiera was now the last mama to have her babies. Two days after Gray Belle had given birth, Kiera had seven beautiful, healthy kittens. Three medium-haired black males, and four torbi females just like her. For three days things were on automatic pilot in the maternity business. Then I came home from an appointment and checked on Kiera, only to find that she wasn't with her babies. She was backed into a corner of the room looking very listless. I picked her up, and she was red hot with fever. I took her right to the animal hospital that I was using at that time. She had a temperature of 105 degrees, and the vet figured she was fighting a bug. So he gave her a Pendex shot, which is a combination of penicillin and a steroid called dexamethasone, to help lower her temperature. We then went back home, but the vet wanted to see her back first thing in the morning. At that point, her fever had dropped a little but not much, so he gave her another shot of Pendex.

This time I took her home and had to leave shortly thereafter for a lecture that I was giving across town. I returned back home at six o'clock that night to find Kiera in bad shape and the babies screaming. I picked Kiera up and discovered that one of her teats was red hot and nasty looking. I knew right then that she had mastitis, an acute infection of the breast. I knew the babies were starving, so I gave one to Vana, three to the feral mama on the sun porch, and three to Gray Belle and just prayed everything would be alright until I could get back home from the emergency vet with Kiera. I flew to the emergency vet as fast as I could because I knew Kiera's life was in major jeopardy. I called ahead to alert them that we needed iced fluids to quickly reduce an extreme temperature. They took her from me right away while I filled out the paperwork. I knew it was going to be very expensive, but I couldn't let her die.

The vet asked me what had happened. I told her that Kiera had been ill and had received two Pendex shots the past two days and that this was how I found her today after the second shot. The vet informed me that the mastitis was bad and that her fever was 107.3 degrees! The Pendex had almost killed her because it had suppressed her immune system by keeping it from rallying against the infection. I don't know how she lived and, to our knowledge, she did not suffer brain damage. She was put on heavy-duty antibiotics, and the next day she was sent home with special instructions. The sad news was that Kiera was unable to nurse her kittens anymore because the mastitis had spread to her other teats. Also, the antibiotics could harm the babies.

I kept Kiera in my room while she recuperated. And, thankfully, all the other surrogate mothers accepted Kiera's babies. This meant that LeAnne had her original five, and Vana, Chloe, and Gray Belle each had seven. That's twenty-six kittens altogether!

Kiera healed nicely, and we ended up keeping her. She was very lucky to be alive after a near fatal medication mistake. We had no idea she had mastitis until it was almost too late. The combination of the penicillin with dexamethasone had completely squashed Kiera's immune system, leaving her vulnerable to the bacterial infection. This was a mistake that any veterinarian could have made because of the nature of the infection, meaning that an infection in the breast or teat isn't always obvious and can easily be missed, therefore misdiagnosed. We call Kiera our one-thousand-dollar kitty!

Kiera

CHAPTER FIVE

De-Stress the Situation before the Situation Stresses You

Sometimes our furry felines can really be a challenge. They seem to know exactly just how to push our buttons and usually at the wrong time. I have seen it all in the past fifteen or so years. They truly are the superior species. Just when you think you've got them figured out, they go and throw you for a loop, and this is their sole mission in life. I think it's their way of getting back at us for domesticating them.

Cats can be our best friend or our worst enemy. They can be extremely loyal but can also betray us in a heartbeat, especially when we dare to bring in a new pet or spouse. They are pros at manipulating us humans to do exactly what they want and when. For example: How many times have you been trying to get something done when your cat just keeps on bothering you? They know when it's close to their feeding time, but you want to finish what you started before you take the time to feed the cat. Suddenly, you can't take it anymore, and you stop what you're doing to feed the cat. And this is exactly what the cat set out to accomplish. They are miniature children used to getting their own way. However, I nipped behaviors such as this in the bud long ago with my cats. If you don't set the guidelines from the get-go, then you are in for an arduous relationship with your feline friend. I will provide some tips to balancing the relationship you have with your cat but tipping the odds in your favor as well.

Before we get started, it is very important that you understand the body language of a cat. If you learn to read him by the way he acts, looks, or sounds, you will be better able to head off potential problems. Here is a list of some of the things your cat is trying to communicate through body language.

BODY LANGUAGE	MEANING
Tail pointing up	Confident, excited, or happy
Limp tail	Relaxed
Tail between the legs	Afraid, unsure, or nervous
Ears turned forward	Friendly, playful, or curious
Ears pulled back	Angry, afraid, has had enough
Pupils dilated	Afraid, traumatized, or anxious
Lying with belly up	Very comfortable, accepting of you, or submissive
Crouched/eyes half-closed	Not feeling well
Third eyelid (cat's protective outer eyelid) raised	Not feeling well
Crouched, ready to pounce	Aggressive or playful
Hair raised or puffed up	Intimidating, afraid, or means business
Head bumps you	Claiming you as his, marking his territory
Rubs against you	Accepting you
Quivering tail	Excited, happy, or spraying
Wagging tail	Intensely concentrated
Thrashing tail	Angry, annoyed
Tail flicking upward	Greeting humans or animals

Hopefully, these explanations of a cat's body language will help you to better understand your cat and his actions. Cats do try to communicate with us on many levels.

Planning a Trip/Boarding Your Cat

Planning a trip can be very stressful on both you and your cat. As soon as cats see your overnight bags come out of the closet, they know that you will be leaving them. I have actually started keeping my suitcase in the closet until the very last moment. If you have a walk-in closet, you can even pack your bags in the closet and leave them there until it is time to leave. This serves two purposes. The first is that it will reduce the amount of time your cat will be stressed prior to your departure. The second is that it will invariably cut down on the amount of hair you will have all over your luggage prior to leaving. A lint roller is always packed in the front pocket of my suitcase expressly to de-hair my luggage.

Some cats will even show their displeasure at your imminent departure by urinating on your bags. This is definitely behavioral. Avoid a bad situation and keep your bags hidden until it is necessary to begin packing, and then place them somewhere where your cat can't get to them.

The next hurdle is what to do with your cat while you are away. You have two choices. You can board your cat at a veterinary practice that offers boarding, a kennel-boarding facility, or one of the newest kinds of animal-lodging services—a kitty bed-and-breakfast (also called a kitty spa). The second choice you have is to hire a pet-sitter. Pet-sitters are listed in the phone book, but better yet, you can usually find one that works at your vet's office. And at the very least, they should be able to recommend someone that is reputable. Ask for references and make sure they are bonded (insured). I personally prefer pet-sitters. It is a lot less stress on your cat and you usually avoid the risk of your cat catching something horrible at the vet or kitty spa. Remember that animals in mass numbers breed disease. Many of these types of boarding places also recommend that you have your cat vaccinated prior to boarding. This is in your cat's best interest because odds are that your cat will get stressed, its immune system will be compromised, and sickness will be the outcome. However, just because your cat has been vaccinated does not mean he won't get sick. You should plan on vaccinating your cat at least two weeks prior to taking him to a kennel facility to give the body time to build up immunity.

Pet-sitters may cost you a little more than boarding would, but to have someone come to your home two to three times daily to take care of your cat is worth it. An average visit runs approximately ten to twelve dollars per trip. So a visit twice daily would cost twenty-four dollars. Some charge less and some more.

There are a few things you can do to make your cat feel more at ease while you're away. I will leave my pajamas and a robe on the bed for them to sleep on while I'm gone. I have found that this cuts down on behavioral issues such as wetting your bed or pillow in your absence. It is the proverbial security blanket for them. Make sure you put away all other items of clothing, especially if they are soiled or need laundering. This includes towels too. Cats will urinate on soiled laundry. If your cat has developed the nasty habit of urinating on your bed whenever you leave him, you can avoid this happening if you use a scat mat, which is an electric mat that gives a small jolt whenever they jump up on it. This changes the behavior eventually. You can also buy a cheap shower curtain liner and cover your bed to protect it. Make sure you put all shoes and slippers away as well because puppies aren't the only chewers of shoes. Cats will chew or gnaw on shoes out of spite or just because they can, just like dogs. I have had numerous pairs of shoes ruined because I left them out while I was away.

Pet-sitters will usually top off the feeding and water bowls, scoop boxes, play with your cat, and make sure all is well in the house. I make it a point to leave extra feeding and water bowls out in the event something should happen to hold up the pet-sitter. It is also a good idea to set out an extra litter box, especially if you have a multiple-cat household. Many pet-sitters will even bring in the mail if you ask them to. It is stressful enough on your cat when you leave him behind, but it truly is easier when he can remain in his own surroundings. I have also made it a point to leave the radio on so there is noise in the house. A few lights should also be left on for security purposes.

In all honesty, most veterinary offices are so busy that your cat might not get much attention at all and will be kept in a kennel cage that is no more than two by two feet. Trust me, there will be heck to pay when you get home if you leave "the superior species" at the vet while you run off to play. However, this being said, there is no guarantee that your cat won't take ill while you're away, whether he is at home or in a kennel, such as in Peanut's case.

Peanut's Story, Part 2—Rhinotracheitis

You all met Peanut in the first chapter. I should have known back then that he was going to be a high-maintenance cat. He is one of the loves of our lives, and we almost lost him for the second time in 2003.

My sister Stephanie was diagnosed with breast cancer back in 2000, and this devastating news rocked our worlds. I threw myself into learning all I could about breast cancer and ended up attending a breast cancer support group called Bosom Buddies. I eventually became a facilitator for the group and whole-heartedly helped to plan our first big fund-raiser. We called it "Cruising For Hope." We booked a three-day cruise to the Bahamas for a large group of breast cancer survivors and family members for October 15, 2003. We were all very excited as we climbed aboard the *Sovereign of the Seas* ship. We booked thirty cabins and raised almost three thousand dollars for the cause. But I have to tell you that, not only was this our first cruise, but it was also the first time we had left our home and pets, which I refer to as "the zoo," with a sitter. Kay happened to be a fellow rescuer and offered to help out while we were away.

Before the trip, Kay came over and met the zoo. I showed her around and left numerous notes of what to do all over the house. After embarking, I called her from ship to shore, which is not cheap, every day and was assured that all was well. On the final day of the cruise, Kay asked me if I'd made other arrangements for Peanut because she didn't recall seeing him at all. I said no, that he was there, and she immediately began searching for him. By this time we were through customs and had just boarded the bus to head back home. That was the longest trip I ever remembered. Two hours dragged by unmercifully. I was very worried about Peanut. Kay could not locate him. When we got home I called for Peanut, and he was nowhere to be found. It was six o'clock on a Sunday night. Finally, I found him under my bed. He was severely dehydrated, hadn't eaten in three days, and had a fever of 105 degrees. I immediately ran him up to the emergency vet. They kept him overnight, gave him fluids, and recommended that I transfer him to the veterinary specialists because they suspected that he swallowed a string or some other foreign object as he was swallowing with great difficulty. To me, it almost looked like he had strep throat and swollen glands.

I took him to the specialists as instructed, and they ran all kinds of tests. I told them it looked like he had a sore throat and a bad cold. I asked them if they thought he had rhinotracheitis. They said that it was highly unlikely because of his recent barrage of vaccines. They continued to do a barium series and more X-rays, looking for the elusive foreign object. At the end of a very long afternoon after numerous expensive tests, the doctor came to me in the waiting room and informed me that Peanut was suffering from rhinotracheitis. I was appalled that they had put him through so many fruitless diagnostics only to discover the obvious. Not to mention that Peanut was now the twelve-hundred-dollar cat. He was prescribed an antibiotic called Orbax, and we went home.

The pet-sitter was not at fault for Peanut's virus. We had over thirty cats for Kay to keep track of, and the stress of us leaving certainly didn't help Peanut to ward off the very tenacious rhinotracheitis virus. Keep in mind that Peanut had more than an ample amount of vaccines that should have protected him. My theory is that, if you have an immune-suppressed cat, such as Peanut, then no vaccine in the world will keep him from getting viruses. This holds true especially if they are prone to chronic viral infections like rhinotracheitis, which is a member of the herpes family of diseases. I personally feel such cats should *not* be vaccinated. Peanut is now five and a half years old and has not been vaccinated since he was a kitten. He's been healthy and has taken on the role in the rescue organization as the nurturer. He loves to take care of the babies. The key to keeping him healthy

Peanut at two years of age with baby Cami

is to keep his immune system healthy. You too can do this for your cat if he is immune-compromised. (See the Holistic Cat Immune-Boosting Formula, Chapter Six.)

If you do decide to board your cat, here are a few suggestions to make your cats stay a lot healthier and less stressed.

- Make sure you send your cat with his favorite bed or blanket so he has familiar smells. An article of your clothing is also a good idea. This, believe it or not, provides a sense of comfort.
- You should also include a few of his favorite toys so he has something to do while he awaits your return. A track ball or track mouse is a good way to keep him entertained.
- Most vets or kennels encourage bringing your cat's favorite food. This way they are not thrown off by being forced to eat whatever it is the facility serves. Make sure you label the container so the staff will know exactly who it belongs to and who should get it. Send a little extra in the event you get detained

another day or two. Also make sure you add the Holistic Cat Immune-Boosting Formula (see Chapter Six) to the food. His immune system can use all the help it can get in a boarding situation.

- If your cat is healthy, then it is in your cat's best interest to have his vaccines brought up to date. If your cat is ever going to catch something, this will be the time. Make sure he is protected from the highly contagious viruses we spoke of earlier. The most common ailment in boarding facilities is conjunctivitis. It is highly contagious and hard to keep in check when dealing with mass numbers. It usually isn't serious, though, and a little eye ointment or Similasan eye drops will usually clear it up. This ailment has been directly linked to stress, and we have seen it firsthand. When we show cats for the first time at Petco or place cats with new foster caregivers, the cats get stressed and will develop runny eyes almost immediately. And by the way vaccines will not protect against conjunctivitis.

- Double check that whoever will be taking care of your cat knows how to reach you in an emergency. All your contact phone numbers, including those of a good friend or family member, should be on file. Don't assume they are—make sure they are. This is just in case something happens to you, and the facility needs to contact someone else.

- Make sure your name is on everything you leave in the vet or kennel's care, such as feed bowls, feed containers, and especially your cat carrier. I can't tell you how many times I left my carrier at the vet with my cat, only to have them send it home with someone else's pet.

- I also tell people to include a cream called Rescue Cream by Bach Flower Essence. This cream simply gets rubbed into the cats' ears, and in moments they feel calm. This would benefit any cat that is easily stressed.

- Finally, if your cat is taking daily medications, it is imperative that you instruct the caregiver explicitly. Never give the facility the full prescription. Count out the number of pills, plus a few extra. When you return, and they give you back what's left, you will know exactly how many pills were actually given to your cat.

I think that about covers it. Knowing that your cat will be in good hands is so important to your well-being and that of your cats too. Check people out and keep in mind that *they* are working for *you*. You will only have peace of mind while you're away if you cover all the bases.

Introducing the New Pet

This can be a real challenge. I will tell you up front that I have been introducing newbies to the existing zoo for many years. It's really funny to me that the experts recommend a slow introduction between the newbie and your other pets. I feel that this method only adds more fuel to the fire by making them stress and wonder who has come into their home. You are really only prolonging the inevitable introduction. Therefore, I believe in "baptism by fire." Do you think for a moment that out in the wild a cat is going to hang back and stay in his own sector, while the other cats come over and smell him and debate whether to accept him or not? Heck no! They are going to strut right in and either get smacked and hissed at or find instant harmony. The latter is usually not the case. The newcomers will more times than not get the cold shoulder treatment and will be kept at bay until the others decide to accept them. This acceptance will usually come in time.

Cats are very clever, and this is why they live in colonies, one dominating the other or others. This is actually a process all animals go through to form what's known as the pecking order. Look at ants, for example. You have the mighty queen, her protectors (soldiers), the scavengers, and all her workers. It's very similar with cats. In your home it's no different. Someone *will* rule the roost, and I do recommend giving it time. Be patient and eventually they will all come to an understanding. Some will become best buddies, and others will only tolerate each other. They are no different then we are in regard to socialization. If you witness a going-for-the-throat vicious attack, *then* you may have a problem. Separate them and gradually introduce them with extreme supervision.

Here are a few guidelines:

1. Leave your new pet in an enclosed room and allow your pet to sniff under the door and play footsies. You can even leave the pet carrier, with the new pet in it, out in the open to see how your other pets will react to the newbie. However, expect hissing as most cats feel cornered when another approaches while they're confined.

2. Sometimes it helps to take a hand towel and rub it all over the new pet. Then take another towel and rub it all over your old pet. Now give the new pet towel to your old pet and vice versa. This allows them to get the other pet's scent before the introduction.

3. *Do not* ignore your existing pet. Pay extra special attention to him so he doesn't feel left out—or worse—like he is being replaced.

4. Keep a spray bottle handy, and don't be afraid to use it when a scuffle breaks out.

5. It may be a good idea to keep your pets separate while you are away just in case a fight should break out. When you feel secure enough to leave them on their own, just make sure the newbie can retreat to a safe zone, like the room he was originally kept in.

6. Whatever you do, *never* let a new cat outdoors until he is very sure of his surroundings. This usually takes two to three

weeks of being kept indoors. Cats rely heavily on smell, and when let outdoors for the first time, nothing is familiar and chances are they will disappear or wander off.

7. As far as the litter box goes, most cats will share their box; however, it certainly doesn't hurt to give the newbie his own. This will usually prevent any behavioral issues associated with a new cat invading the other cats' territory. And do the same with feeding bowls. Don't expect your cat to be happy about sharing his feeding bowl with another cat. Give them each their own bowls.

Earlier, I urged you to make sure that you don't ignore your other cat while you are introducing the newbie. Female cats especially will feel they are being replaced. The new cat will have lots to explore and isn't going to miss your affections during this process. This is the time to pay special attention to your old cat and honor his feelings. Do not reprimand for bad behavior, but instead reward for good behavior. However, if the cat or dog is misbehaving and causing harm, then most certainly intervene. Do this in one of three ways:

1. A firm *no* and a loud handclap will usually give them the signal that you are displeased.
2. Keep a squirt bottle handy, and use it when the pets are getting aggressive.
3. Fill a soda pop can with some coins then seal the opening with duct tape. Throw this can near the altercation, and it will definitely break up a fight. *Do not* make it too heavy as you can knock your cat out if you miss your mark. It's the sound that the can makes when it hits the floor that breaks the behavioral pattern.

Never hit your cat. Cats remember. You can risk the cat developing trust issues, and it will take you a long time to re-establish that trust. The last thing you want is for your cat to fear you. Spare the rod is the way to go—at least for cats.

When you have as many cats as I do, you are bound to have at least one or two personality conflicts. I have one male cat named Pretty Boy (whom I previously talked about) that has an unhealthy hatred for Tessa. Tessa is a bi-eyed (one blue and one green) buff tabby that is very sweet and not quite all there. She can only see out of her green eye, and while she was in the colony (before we rescued her) she was hit by a car and was never the same after that. Tessa was hit in the back end and thrown landing on her head and neck. She healed, although we still consider her one of our special needs cats. I believe this is why Pretty Boy picks on her. Being an alpha (cat version of top dog), it is typical to pick on the weakest one. Because of his hatred toward her, I have to keep them separated. This is the only personality conflict we have amongst the zoo.

Now there is a completely different protocol when introducing a cat to a dog or vice versa. The dog must be restrained on a leash during this process and must immediately be taught not to chase a running cat. You do this by jerking the leash backwards and telling the dog *no* sharply. It takes only a second for a cat to sustain a crushing bite that can kill him instantly or cause internal bleeding and injury. The dog and cat must always be supervised until you know that they will get along.

My dog Jack was raised with cats and kittens. Being a rescued dog himself, he has always been around other rescued animals. He is a gentle giant. Jack is a yellow lab and is now fourteen years old. I have never had an incident involving Jack and cats or kittens. However, one day I let Jack outside because he was crying at the door. He flew out the door, ran across the yard, and plucked a baby raccoon right off a tree as it was fleeing from him. I had followed closely behind but was too late. Jack crushed him immediately in his jaws. I was devastated. This was a classic example of the thrill of the chase. I know Jack didn't mean to kill the little guy, but in his exuberance he did. No matter how gentle and sweet a dog is, it is a natural part of his entire being to be in pursuit of whatever may be running in front of him. A child, cat, rabbit, or another dog will inspire the game of chase if they start running.

This is why we tell children not to run from a stray dog. Children should always stand still and cover their face, bringing all limbs in close. Unfortunately, animals don't know this rule, and they run like heck, which in turn officially commences the game of chase.

Moving/Relocation Procedures

As a rescue organization, we have heard many stories of cat owners losing their cats after relocating to a new area. Most people don't realize that cats need plenty of time to adjust to their new surroundings. They do not like being uprooted, and most cats do not tolerate change very well either. Like most humans, cats feel safe when in an environment with familiar smells, sounds, and people. When they are taken from their safe zone, they experience stress and anxiety, and some will even develop depression, which I will discuss in the following section. Moving can be very traumatic to your cat. Below are some helpful tips to make your moving experience easier on you and your cat.

> TIP #1—*Relocating procedure.* It is of the utmost importance that you keep your cat contained indoors for at least two to three weeks after moving into your new home. If you let him outside any earlier than this, he will more than likely disappear. You can keep an outdoor cat enclosed in a screened-in sun porch; however, he may climb the screens, and you may suffer some damage to your porch. It is best to have an enclosure built to contain him. You can use a garage, but you run the risk of someone opening the door and the cat escaping. Large kennels work just as well as long as they are protected from the elements and predators. Your cat may feel more secure being kept indoors for awhile. Once things fall into place and he gets more comfortable with his new surroundings, only then is

the time to let him explore the outside. Supervision is required until you are absolutely sure he knows where he lives and that he will not run away. Dogs will try to find their way back to what they know, but I am not sure cats have this ability. I have heard that they do but have not witnessed this firsthand.

TIP #2—*Traveling.* If you plan on flying with your cat, make sure you check with the airlines in advance to make sure there is room on board for your cat. Most flights will only allow two pets per flight. Your cat must be in an FAA-approved carrier, and it has to fit under your seat. Do not allow your pet to be stowed in the cargo section of the plane. This is extremely traumatic for your cat because of the temperature changes as well as the noise. You must also have a health certificate from your vet stating that the cat is in good health and is up to date on all vaccines. The same goes for rail and ship. When traveling, it might be good to have a prescription of Prozac for your cat, especially if your cat is the nervous type. I actually prefer Rescue Cream by Bach Flower remedy. This cream will do the same thing Prozac will do, only naturally. Simply massage the cream into your cat's ears and he will be immediately calmed. This will enable your cat to relax and snooze. It is also a good idea to purchase a pop-up kennel cage for the car. Carriers can be very close quarters for a cat, and most won't accommodate a litter box, whereas a kennel cage will. Place the cage in the backseat with an attachable water bowl and food dish and a small litter box with just enough litter to cover the bottom of the box. You can also include a small hooded bed for your cat to snuggle in and feel safe while traveling in the kennel cage. When you reach your destination or hotel, take the entire cage out of the car and carry it into the house or hotel. This will ensure that your cat doesn't have a chance to escape while transferring him to his new or temporary home. I usually put the cage in a bathroom and open the cage door but close the bathroom door so the cat is contained. This is a good idea because, if you have movers coming and going, odds are the cat will freak out and could possibly run out an open door. The same goes for a strange hotel room. It is better to keep him confined than chance his getting loose and running out an open door. He will feel more secure in a confined space.

TIP #3—*Give him his own space.* Whatever you do, don't give your cat the entire house when you both arrive at your new home. He must be given a small, safe, protected area in the house where he will feel secure. Be sure to give him his bed, toys, and other familiar items. A master closet, small bedroom, or your bedroom are good choices. Let him get used to one area first before you let him roam the entire house. If he wants to hide under the bed, let him. If he won't come out of hiding other than to eat or use the litter box for a few days, that's okay. It is perfectly normal for a cat to be afraid and angry at you for disrupting his life, and he will come around on his own terms. Be patient, and things will get back to normal in time.

TIP #4—*Attitude adjustment.* If you have other pets, don't be surprised if they hiss and smack each other while exploring their new territories. All the new unfamiliar smells will throw them off. Did you ever take your cat to the vet and bring him home only to have your other cat or dog hiss or growl at him? This is normal because of the new smells on your cat from being at the vet. The same goes for new homes. Give your cat plenty of time to adjust, and his attitude will adjust accordingly; however, as mentioned, a new home comes with new smells. A cat will more than likely mark his territory in the new home, especially if there are other animal smells there. Animal scents caused from previous animals are a threat to your cat; therefore, he must make it a point to make those areas his by marking them. A cat will either scratch or spray to mark territory. Cats have sweat glands, also called scent glands, that are in the pads of their feet. They secrete a hormone, and this is how they mark their territory when scratching. The other ways they mark their area are by urinating or spraying.

I want to take a moment to discuss the inhumane act of de-clawing a cat. I have found that cats that have been de-clawed will not only urinate or spray to mark their territory because they no longer have their claws, but will also turn to biting as their defense system. Many families will de-claw their cat because of young children in the house and then find that the cat will now bite when being mishandled. A cat generally will not scratch the first time he swipes at you. He will bat you with his paw without using his claws. Cats will only use claws when in a defensive situation, as this is their first line of defense. When the surgical procedure is performed to remove the claws of a cat, it is actually considered an amputation. The claws are not the only things cut off. The nail grows into the first knuckle of the cat's toes, so it too is removed. This is a terrible thing to do to a cat. You can train your cat not to scratch furniture by giving him ample things to scratch such as variegated cardboard, sisal scratch posts or pads, and wood posts. Spray these items with catnip to attract your cat so he will know it is his to scratch. To learn more about de-clawing your cat, please visit www.declawing.com.

I have never had much luck concerning the cats I call "carpet urinators." And this problem is why I am a firm believer that carpet and cats don't mix. I truly believe that cats urinate on carpet because the chemicals used in the manufacturing process of carpet are estrogenic. My theory is that cats, both male and female, smell or sense the estrogenic chemicals in the carpet and are therefore attracted to it. Estrogen is present in a female cat's urine, even in small amounts after being spayed. In turn, urinating on carpet seems a natural thing to do. Think about cats when they use the litter box—they rely heavily on smell and will search for the scent of urine before urinating. I myself have discovered that females will urinate on carpet; however, males will oftentimes spray on the carpet to mark their territory because of the scent of the female hormone estrogen.

I have replaced the carpet in an entire house only to have my cats urinate on it all over again. This is when I began researching the composition of carpet. If you have a throw rug that has no backing on it, odds are that a cat will not urinate on it, especially if it is made from cotton or wool and is not synthetic. Many synthetic (man-made) materials, especially those that are comprised of rubber, latex, or plastics in general, are considered to be estrogenic. These chemicals are called xenoestrogens or endocrine-disrupting chemicals, and plastics and rubber products, like the backing on carpet, fall into this category. Every other type of carpeting, including bath mats, are to be considered cat-attractive as well. If you love your cat and want to keep him inside only, then I highly suggest either closing off the rooms in your house that are carpeted or get rid of the carpet altogether. However, I must tell you that most of the coatings used on wood floors, like polyurethane, are also made from estrogenic chemicals. I have had a few female cats urinate on my wood floors. This is not a common problem, though, because cats generally like to bury their business, and a wood floor or hard surface doesn't allow for this. Carpet is much more desirable to cats.

I have heard that the pheromone products, such as Feliway, that are available at pet stores will deter urinating and spraying on the floors. I have not tried these products myself. Over the years, out of dozens of cats, we only had four that continued to spray no matter what we did to deter them. One was a male and three were females. Yes, females spray too. These cats ended up being moved outside to end the problem in the house. I have found that this spraying will usually happen in two kinds of cats: those cats that have the alpha personality and those that are loners. We have a cat named Cindy Lou that is very independent. She loves the dogs but hates other cats. She would continually mark territories all over the house. Cindy Lou adjusted very well to being an outside cat since we could not break her of this bothersome spraying habit. Our male cat, Tiger, sprayed everywhere and was definitely an alpha male. He too joined Cindy Lou outside. If putting your cat outside isn't an option because of busy roads, then I recommend trying the cat-hormonal products I mentioned earlier. I believe Feliway is a good product and is available at most pet stores. I finally got rid of the problem of cats urinating on carpet by getting rid of all carpet. Again, I stress that cats and carpet don't mix.

With patience and time your cat will adjust to his new home and things will return to normal.

Depression in Cats

I have seen depression in cats firsthand. Many people believe that cats do not experience human-like emotion. I am not one of those people as I see proof everyday of the contrary. Cats experience happiness, sorrow, anger, joy, jealousy, hatred, and definitely depression, especially when associated with separation anxiety. As a rescue agency, we see this depression in cats more often than not because of all the adoptions we do. We have certain cats or kittens that must be adopted with a sibling or friend.

Rosie (nicknamed CB which stands for crybaby) and Ross are prime examples. CB and Ross came to me as four-week-old babies. They had three other litter mates as well. Race and Rena were adopted together when they were nine weeks of age. Shortly thereafter their sister Rachel took ill and died within a week. She had a congenital heart defect. The night she died, Ross and CB never left her side and stayed physically touching her until she passed. All the cats in the house came over and sniffed her and lay with her as well.

From that day on CB and Ross stuck together like glue. They are both black-and-white tuxedo cats, and when Ross was three months old, I adopted him out to a single man. Tom was not interested in adopting two kittens, so we agreed to let him have Ross without CB. Two weeks later we got Ross back. He wasn't eating well, had lost weight, had developed a mild upper respiratory infection from stress, which left him in a weakened immune state, and he had pretty much lived under Tom's bed. Ross was suffering greatly from depression. Everything he had known was gone—including his sister. There were no familiar smells or sounds around to comfort him. Tom hated giving up on Ross, but I knew Ross missed his sister terribly and that was why he took ill.

I'll never forget Ross and CB's reunion. They would not leave each other alone, and I vowed that they would stay together from that point on. During the Christmas adoptions CB and Ross were adopted out to a family together. They did very well for two weeks, then Ross got sick again. This time he was really sick. It turns out that they took CB to the vet for a nail trim then continued on to visit friends for several hours. Ross ran and hid when he saw the carrier come out for their trip to the vet, so he was left behind. This stressed Ross beyond imagination. By the time they returned with CB, Ross was lethargic and feverish and wouldn't eat, so naturally they separated them again in order to protect CB from whatever Ross had.

The next day the family called me because the vet was closed and told me their predicament. I offered to take both cats back in order to care for Ross. When I got them to my home, his fever had spiked to 106.7 degrees. I placed Ross in a small cat carrier with a blanket and packed ice bags under the blanket all around him. This is a good way to quickly cool down a cat. I also gave him fluids and kept him by my side throughout the night.

His fever broke early the next morning. After that point, I kept CB and Ross together knowing that she was already exposed to whatever Ross had. And CB was the best medicine for Ross. She cleaned him continually and stayed by his side as if she were watching over him. He recovered fully within two days, and CB never broke with whatever was ailing Ross. I called their owners to give them the good news, and they were thrilled but decided not to take CB and Ross back because they would have been devastated had Ross died. The reason they came to us for a cat in the first place was because their former

CB and Ross

cat had died suddenly for unknown reasons. I still have CB and Ross today.

We alert new adopters that a new home will initially stress most pets, and stress causes the immune system to crash. As a result sickness can develop immediately, and in cats it is usually upper respiratory disease. We see this more times then we'd like to admit. They will usually fully recover and adjust quite well to their new home. I honestly believe this occurs, in part, due to depression or separation anxiety. Most of the cats and kittens that we adopt out have been kept with other cats or kittens. We just don't have the space to keep cats completely isolated from one another. And, truthfully, we wouldn't want to. We only isolate those that are sick or in the initial quarantine period when we receive them into the organization. Cats are social creatures and love to be around other animals. So when these kittens go to new homes, leaving everything they've known thus far behind, especially their siblings, many will get depressed. They won't eat or drink much, will hide someplace where they feel safe, and some may even show aggression. I have learned this to be true with mama cats as well. When all their babies are adopted, and the mama cat is left alone, oftentimes she will cry at night and frantically search for her babies. This is why we try our hardest to adopt the mama cat out with at least one of her babies. One of the mama cats we took in suffered from severe depression on a few occasions; her name is Kiki, and this is her story.

Kiki's Story—Post-Partum Depression

Kiki is a beautiful Siamese and tabby mix with the bluest eyes you've ever seen. She was brought to me by a local trapper named Lee Conway. Lee is known for trapping feral cats and transporting them to local veterinarians or spay/neuter clinics such as First Coast No More Homeless Pets (FCNMHP). I believe she is single-handedly responsible for spaying and neutering at least half the feral cat population in Jacksonville.

One day, while trapping out in McClenney, she found Kiki and called me. The cat appeared to be extremely friendly, and Lee suspected that she was also pregnant. She was obviously previously owned and was too sweet to go through the feral cat program. We had a vet check her out and discovered that she was around ten months of age and approximately three to four weeks pregnant. A cat's gestation period is sixty-three to sixty-eight days or a little over two months. I set Kiki up in the nursery, and she made herself very much at home. She wasn't very happy by herself, so I would let her have visiting time with a few of my cats during the day. This made her very happy. She started eating more and playing with the other cats and settled in quite nicely. I estimated that we were about a month or so from the delivery of her kittens.

Her pregnancy was uneventful, and everything seemed to be fine. I started to worry when she went a full week past her due date, though. She had also started passing dark brown discharge. I took her up to the vet and was told that the discharge was normal and that she was about ready to deliver. The vet was concerned, though, because the babies felt small.

Three days later Kiki gave birth. She was struggling, and I was glad I was there to help her. One by one she delivered the babies and cleaned them, not realizing they were all stillborn. I was so worried about her because I had to take them away from her once I knew they were dead. She had six babies. I kept her in my room that night because she was so depressed. She refused to eat or drink and was very lethargic yet wouldn't sleep.

The next morning I took her in to the vet to have her examined. The vet thought that she may have been exposed to one of the feline viruses, and some of them are known to inhibit the growth of fetuses. He also put her on a mild antibiotic because of the discharge. I took her home, and for three days she stayed the same. Kiki only came out of her box to use the litter box and still refused to eat.

That afternoon I got a call from the vet who asked if I would take a couple of two-week-old orphaned kittens whose mother was hit by a car that morning. I immediately thought of Kiki. I went right up to the vet and brought them back to Kiki. She was amazing. She heard them crying as I was carrying them to her, and she was waiting at the door for me as I came down the hall. I put them in her box, and she began to clean them while the kittens nursed. Kiki's depressed state vanished instantly. I had to put the food dish right next to her because after a few hours I'd noticed that she hadn't left the box. Kiki devoured the wet food and salmon I offered her. She was so happy to finally have babies to take care of. The kittens came with the names Lucky and Fancy. Lucky was an orange tabby and Fancy was a torti.

The following week I took in three more orphans around the same age as Lucky and Fancy. Kiki didn't even hesitate and took them as if they were her own. She was the best mother to these orphans, and I wasn't worried until the babies were old enough for adoption. Three of the five kittens got adopted the first week we showed them, leaving only Fancy and Lucky because I wanted them to go to a new home together. I knew the odds were slim to none for placing the kittens and Kiki together.

That Wednesday I got a rescue call from a very distraught woman. She told me that her trailer park was being demolished, and every time they pulled another trailer out, more kittens were found. When all was said and done, there were thirteen kittens ranging between four and six weeks of age. I was her only hope because no one else would help her. I told her I would take them all. She brought them to me that afternoon, and they were in pretty poor shape. Some looked half starved, covered with fleas, infested with worms, and needed a lot of TLC. My husband and I proceeded to bathe them all. Several hours later we put them on the enclosed sun-porch in three different playpens. We separated them by size and state of health. Some looked worse then others. I called this group of kittens the C litter. There was Clyde, Clarence, Clarisse, Chloe, Cody, Cassie, Calvin, Candy, Callie, Carson, Cara, Cory, and Clara. I checked them all for leukemia, and they were all clear. I knew they could really use Kiki's TLC, but I was hesitant to mix her with all these kittens in case they were sick. And I had to think about Fancy and Lucky's welfare as well.

Kiki's nursery room door opened out to the sunporch and as soon as they all started crying, she went nuts. I let this go on until I couldn't bear to hear her talking to them through the door anymore. It was 2:00 a.m., and I was exhausted. I left Fancy and Lucky in the nursery as they were fully weaned and were now about ten weeks old. I opened the door to the sunporch and let Kiki out. She walked around and peered into the three pens, talking to the kittens the whole time. I figured she'd jump in and visit with them during the night. I took Fancy and Lucky in to bed with me.

The next morning I woke up and immediately ran out to check on Kiki and the kittens. I panicked when I saw the first two empty playpens. The third had been pushed away from the wall, and the blanket had been pulled through the bars to the back of the pen. When

I looked behind the pen, there was Kiki with all thirteen kittens! Some were nursing, some were sleeping, and she was diligently cleaning another. I was amazed that she pulled all the kittens out of their pens and took them under her wing, keeping them all together.

For two months she took care of those kittens. Fancy and Lucky were adopted together to a lovely couple, and one by one all of the C litter also got homes. Kiki was adopted to a woman who fell in love with her, but a week later I got her back. Kiki did not adjust to being in a home without her babies. She lost weight and once again fell into depression. I took her to Petco the following week with the hopes of finding a home with multiple cats, and if that didn't work, I would just keep her myself.

Cody (one of the C litter kittens) was adopted by the Jenney family, a large family with lots of children and pets. They came into Petco to adopt a kitten for their son, Austen. Cody was a very special kitten as he had cerebellum disorder and wobbled when he walked. This didn't bother Austen at all. He could have chosen a perfectly healthy kitten, but he fell in love with Cody. When Caroline, the mother of this wonderful family came into Petco for supplies, she saw Kiki and inquired about her. I told her that she was the mama cat that raised Cody and explained Kiki's history. Caroline and I were both emotional over her situation. It was obvious that Kiki missed her babies. Caroline walked outside, made a call, came back in, and informed me that she was taking Kiki home to be with Cody and her family. She said she spoke to her husband to get the go ahead to bring Kiki home. She achieved this by stating that their son Beau didn't have a pet of his own, so she decided to even things out amongst the children by bringing Kiki home for Beau. We were all thrilled for Kiki and Beau! There wasn't a dry eye in the store. Kiki was reunited with her adopted baby. Cody and Kiki couldn't have been placed in a better home. Caroline informed me a few weeks later that Kiki was beginning to put weight back on and was settling in nicely.

Cats experience emotions just as we do and for the same reasons as we do. Don't let anyone tell you otherwise. We could stand to learn so much from these intelligent, beautiful creatures.

Kiki

Cody "up close and personal"

CHAPTER SIX

Disease-Specific Protocols
for Optimal Health

Perfect health is not an easy thing to acquire these days for both humans and animals. The water we drink, the air we breathe, the food we eat, the medications we take, and the stress we endure on a daily basis are all promoters of disease. No one person or animal is exempt from disease. However, more promoters of health in our life and that of our cats will determine our overall health picture. This chapter will give you my recommendations for health-promoting protocols pertaining to specific diseases, as well as an immune-boosting protocol formulated to help stave off disease.

As you know by now, cats are afflicted with many of the same disorders and diseases that humans also have. Oftentimes, treatment plans will be the same for both humans and animals, usually with much smaller doses for animals. This holds true whether your cat is being treated conventionally or holistically. For example, a human with chronic herpes infection would take 500 mg of L-lysine three times daily to keep the virus in remission, whereas a cat will only get 125–250 mg twice daily (depending on weight). However, I must say this does not mean that all human medications or treatments are safe for cats. Many medications can be fatal to a cat. You should always consult your cat's health care practitioner before administering any medication or treatment.

Immune-Building Protocol

Introducing new foster cats and kittens always runs the risk of bringing in disease. No matter how careful we are, there are certain viruses that are transferred via clothing, shoes, and even the air duct system in our homes. As I mentioned before, my household cats are always on my health maintenance formula just to make sure they stay healthy. Whenever I take in a new litter of kittens that are infected with upper respiratory infection, I swap my household over to my immune-boosting formula. This will boost their natural defenses and hopefully ward off any viruses. The immune-boosting formula is very simple to make. Here is the recipe:

The Holistic Cat Immune-Boosting Formula

7,500 mg L-lysine tablets (crushed or in powdered form)

3,000 mg vitamin C powder

1,500 mg bromelain (crushed)

200 mg vitamin B6 tablets (crushed)

750 mg odorless garlic (capsules)

¼ cup ground flaxseed (source of vitamin E)

Preparation:

Mix all ingredients together and divide into thirty doses, then store in an airtight container in a dark place.

Dosage:

Give one dose to healthy cats during the course of an outbreak to boost immune function.

Dosage:

Give one dose twice daily to cats that are already ill.

L-lysine, which is an amino acid, aids in the production of antibodies, hormones, and enzymes, making it very important for immune function. Vitamin C is an important antioxidant that decreases the susceptibility to disease. Vitamin B6 aids the absorption of L-lysine and vitamin C, making these three supplements a powerhouse combination. Garlic boosts immune function and contains antioxidants, such as vitamins A and C and selenium. Flaxseed and bromelain both have anti-inflammatory properties and aid digestion. Proper digestion is essential for immune function. Keep in mind that 80 percent of the immune system is housed in the gut, and it is of vital importance to keep the digestive system on track and running smoothly.

There are two ways to maintain the integrity of the gut. The first is by taking digestive enzymes. For my cats I use a product by PetGuard called Natural Digestive Enzyme Blend for Cats. It contains bromelain, amylase, cellulase, lipase, protease, phytase, alpha-galactosidase, acidophilus, bifidus, and calcium (to enhance uptake or absorption). PetGuard only uses human-grade ingredients in their pet products. This product, or digestive enzymes in general, assists the digestive system with the breakdown of food. All pets would benefit greatly with the addition of digestive enzymes to their food, especially those that are immune-challenged or have diabetes. Diabetes is the result of the pancreas malfunctioning. The body is unable to produce enough insulin, and usually the necessary enzymes and hormones for digestion, thus impeding the digestive process. This is where digestive enzymes will help.

The second way to maintain the integrity of the gut is by taking probiotics, which I just briefly mentioned. PetGuard at this time doesn't have a product for probiotics specifically. However, the digestive enzyme product they offer does contain some probiotics. I usually purchase probiotics that contain acidophilus and bifidus only because there are other forms of bacteria that are sometimes added to probiotics that would not be compatible with cats' digestive system. Nature's Way makes a good product called Primadophilus. Probiotics are also added to the food but should be stored in the refrigerator. Open the capsule and sprinkle a small amount over the food. Probiotics are simply friendly bacteria that help restore balance in the gut. They are vital for proper digestion and also prevent the overgrowth of yeast and other pathogens. Everyone can benefit from probiotics, and I will give you more uses for them in the next section.

In summary, my immune-building protocol is:

- One serving of the Holistic Cat Immune-Boosting Formula daily, as directed
- Digestive enzymes daily, as directed
- Probiotics daily, as directed

Now I want to give you a few protocols for specific disorders or diseases beginning with upper respiratory infections.

Upper Respiratory Infections—URIs

Upper respiratory infections, also called URIs, can be very difficult to clear up because most times they are of viral origin, not bacterial. As you know from the previous chapters, viruses cannot be treated with antibiotics. Supportive therapies are the best course of treatment. I mentioned before that antibiotics cause neutropenia (white blood cell depletion), leukopenia (white blood cell depletion), and thrombocytopenia (red blood cell depletion). Antibiotics destroy the very cells that are necessary for fighting off the virus. This is why cats will oftentimes get worse after beginning a course of antibiotics. When a secondary infection (that is bacterial) is suspected, then antibiotics will come into play. I have to tell you that this is rare; I have seen few cases of a secondary bacterial infection developing while treating a viral infection.

Symptoms associated with an upper respiratory infection are watery, runny, and crusty eyes, nasal congestion, runny nose, fever, lethargy (unusually tired), joint aches, coughing, sneezing, and sometimes mouth sores. The herpes virus is usually the culprit behind these infections.

The first thing you must do is isolate the cat from other cats in the household. These viruses are usually contagious only within the species (cat to cat), but I must tell you that humans get rhinotracheitis (one of the upper respiratory viruses). I'll swear that I've gotten sick several times while taking care of kittens that had it, so make sure you wash your hands frequently.

It is important to know if your cat is running a fever. Taking a cat's temperature is not very difficult. A rectal thermometer (digital is faster) placed in the rectum only takes a few seconds. Most cats that are ill will not fight this. Have someone hold the cat on a flat surface like the bed or sofa. Lay the cat on her side and scratch under her chin or at the back of her head to relax her. With a little petroleum jelly on the end of the thermometer, lift the tail and insert it about one half inch. This is far enough to get a good reading. Don't panic when you see the temperature soar over 104 degrees. The normal temperature for a cat is between 101.7 and 102 degrees. Stress can slightly elevate a cat's temperature, and I usually will not intervene until it goes over 106. A fever is the body's natural defense system attempting to kill the virus.

TREATING A FEVER

Fluids are the most important supportive therapy when treating a fever. Pedialyte (plain) for children is a good thing to have on hand when your cat takes ill. You can purchase this at your local pharmacy. While you're there, pick up a 3-ml and a 6-ml syringe (no needle attached). Draw the Pedialyte up into the syringe, offer it to your cat by placing the syringe into the side of her mouth, and slowly dispense. I like to add a little tuna juice from a can packed in water. This makes for a stronger taste. Be very careful not to aspirate. Plunging too fast can cause the fluid to get sucked into her lungs. Do this every few hours if she is dehydrated. You can tell this by pinching the skin at the back of her neck (the scruff), and if it sticks and takes a few seconds to go back down, she is dehydrated. If her temperature soars over 106, then you should seek medical attention. If there isn't anyone available, then you must try to cool her down. Do this by placing your cat into her carrier or travel cage and on a folded towel with ice packs (two or three should be sufficient) under the first layer of the towel, making sure they are all around her and not directly on her. This will be uncomfortable for her, and she will try to get up and get off them. By placing the ice packs around her, the temperature will radiate throughout the carrier and keep her cool, thus reducing her temperature.

I will also use miso paste mixed with a little bit of warm water in between fluid feedings. This is very nutritious—packed with vital nutrients and cats seem to like it. Once the fever subsides, your cat can come out of the carrier. Try to entice her with a good brand of canned food mixed with a little water. When she resumes eating, that usually means she is out of the woods and on the mend.

NASAL CONGESTION

Many times a cat will lose her appetite due to nasal congestion because her nose is too stuffed up to smell food. She may also refuse to drink because of this. Little Noses decongestant or saline solution will help to alleviate some of the congestion. Simply scruff the neck, tilt the cat's head back, and drop one drop in each nostril. If she blows it out, repeat the process. Be very careful with other nasal sprays as many have not been approved for use for cats. A humidifier also helps to break up congestion. I would say that nasal congestion can be the most dangerous symptom because cats can't go very long without food and water. This is when you may need to entice her with stronger-smelling foods. Solid Gold makes a canned tuna that is very fishy-smelling. Canned salmon or mackerel purchased at your local grocer is also good. Hill's Science Diet makes a canned food called AD and that mixed with Pedialyte is a good solution to force-feed with a syringe, if necessary. Serious complications can arise from dehydration, so make sure your cat stays well hydrated.

Winston, who we also call Pooh Bear, is a beautiful orange tabby tuxedo. He is now seven months old, and for the past five months he has been on medications, herbal remedies, immune-building supplements, and homeopathics. Pooh Bear has a very tenacious bacterial infection called pseudomonas. It is pretty much antibiotic resistant with the exception of only three drugs. The drug of choice in treating cats for this kind of infection is ciprofloxacin. The infection in Pooh Bear's case is in his right sinus cavity, which makes it nearly impossible to treat. I have successfully kept it at bay but cannot get rid of it completely. He has now been on ciprofloxacin for eleven days with little to no improvement. Today, I decided to try probiotics intranasally, as well as internally (which he's already been on throughout his course of treatment). I opened a capsule of probiotics and dissolved the contents in two to three tablespoons of sterile water. I will use this solution as a nasal flush for his sinuses three times daily or for as long as he'll tolerate it. He is so over people putting stuff in his nose. He was on nose drops for a month and hated it. I will keep you posted on his progress throughout the remainder of the book.

Probiotics can be used in several applications, not only orally. They can be used rectally or vaginally in humans for bacterial or yeast infections. They can also be applied to infectious wounds, and I have even seen people use them topically for fungal infections. Probiotics are probably the most underrated miracle cure we have in medicine

Pooh Bear

today. Anytime an antibiotic is prescribed, a probiotic should also be prescribed. Right now there is a probiotic that doctors prescribe, but it is a pharmaceutical product. Meaning that it probably has a lot of unnecessary ingredients as well, otherwise they wouldn't be able to patent the formula. You see, probiotics are naturally occurring bacteria, and you cannot patent something that's natural.

I am happy to report that we have never lost a kitten or cat to upper respiratory disease. Try these natural remedies before resorting to medication.

Ollie and Hardy's Story—Death Row Rescue

I was sitting at my computer one day when I was alerted that I had e-mail. When I opened my inbox, I was saddened to see a message from our local Animal Care and Control Agency (AC&C). I knew the news wasn't going to be good. They had just taken in two black-and-white twin brothers approximately three months of age with a bad upper respiratory infection. They were due to be put down humanely at four o'clock that day. It was 2:30 p.m. Taking cats that are sick from a shelter results in a lot of heartache, and they require round-the-clock care if they are to live. I was tired, having just finished up a month of bottle feeding a litter of kittens every two to three hours daily. I had actually had my first full night's sleep the previous night as this litter had graduated to eating on their own. I looked at the pictures on my computer of the brothers about to be euthanized staring back at me. I grabbed my purse and headed downtown to AC&C. By the time I got there, there was another kitten also stricken with URI and added to the "kill" list. He was a medium-haired orange tabby named Garfield, of course. He appeared to be the same age as the brothers. I took all three into my care.

As soon as I got them home, I started up the humidifier to help with their nasal congestion. Because they also had lung issues, we decided to start them on Zithromax and a probiotic. These were extremely sick kittens. I had to force feed all of them and give them additional fluids every two to three hours. The fluids were administered orally at first, but little Garfield ended up needing IV fluids as well.

For two weeks their condition seemed to be at a standstill. I was at a loss. They weren't responding to the antibiotic, although they had begun eating on their own after day three. The congestion seemed better but wasn't completely gone. I gave them another three days of Zithromax, and by week three they finally started clearing up. They had a very tenacious rhinotracheitis. When present in a cat with a fairly healthy immune system, rhinotracheitis will last seven to ten days. But when you have kittens that have been stressed to the max by being trapped and put through the process at AC&C, the virus gets a hold and just won't let go. They had every symptom that could possibly be associated with rhinotracheitis. Each morning I had to bathe all their eyes because they were all glued shut from severe conjunctivitis. It took me a full month of giving Ollie, Hardy, and Garfield my full arsenal to get rid of their URIs.

The two brothers were adopted together into a lovely home, and Garfield was adopted into a family that had already rescued a six-month-old puppy. The old adage, "All's well that ends well," seems apropos for this story.

These little guys hold a special place in my heart because I prayed so hard and often for them to be spared, especially after having dodged the bullet of euthanasia at AC&C. My prayers were answered and these kittens beat the odds and survived to brighten the lives of their new families.

Joint Pain and Muscle Aches

As far as modern medicine goes, there isn't a whole lot to be done for cats suffering from inflammatory pain. I have found that bromelain, which is an enzyme found in pineapple, reduces inflammation within the body. Turmeric is an ancient spice and member of the ginger family.

It has many medicinal properties including its pain-killing effect by reducing inflammation. It is also an anti-cancer agent. There is a product available by Solaray that contains both bromelain and turmeric (called Bromelain with Turmeric), and is available in capsule form. Bromelain has blood-thinning properties and can be dangerous to animals if given in excess. Turmeric has had reports of liver problems when taken in excessive amounts. I have successfully used a quarter of one of these caplets per ten-pound cat to alleviate pain. I mix it with one milliliter of tuna juice and administer orally via a syringe. You can also quarter a 500-mg caplet of bromelain, crush it, and sprinkle it on food. I have never had a problem with either product. Both are also great digestive aids. We have recently learned that calcium helps the absorption of bromelain, thus boosting the effects.

Another easy way to soothe your cat's muscle and joint aches is a heating pad or hot water bottle. Cats seem to like the warmth of a heating pad when they are achy and suffering joint discomfort from viral infections. However, it is extremely important *not* to put a cat on a heating pad if she has a fever. As long as there is no fever present, place a heating pad under a towel and turn on to medium heat. Never use high heat. If the cat chooses to lie on it, she will.

Conjunctivitis (Eye Inflammation)

Conjunctivitis, especially in young cats and kittens, is fairly easy to treat but is highly contagious. If the eye is glued shut due to excess discharge, you should take a cotton ball dipped in sterile warm water and gently clean the eye until it opens. Never force an eyelid open that is glued shut. Warm water works like a charm. Then apply a homeopathic eye remedy called Similasan. Try to purchase the one that contains silver sulphate. I believe it is the one that is specific to pink eye or conjunctivitis. Place one to two drops in each affected eye until symptoms subside, then treat for one more day. You can administer these drops two to three times daily. This is a natural remedy as opposed to antibiotic eye ointments that are petroleum based, which can sometimes aggravate the eyes, oftentimes worsening the condition. Most cases of conjunctivitis are of viral origin, not bacterial. Remember what we learned about antibiotics and viral infections? The two do not go together.

Kidney Health

More cats over the age of seven die from kidney failure than from any other disorder. Kidney failure results from the breakdown of the kidneys, usually caused by a serious infection, kidney disease, cancer, or exposure to toxic chemicals. Kidney failure is also common in elderly cats. Whatever the cause may be, it is difficult to treat. I refer to kidney failure as "the effect of the cause." Something caused the kidneys to fail, and the whole key to treating or reversing kidney failure is to find out what caused it in the first place. With the exception of a defective kidney from birth, a kidney doesn't just decide to fail.

I strongly believe one of the major contributors to kidney failure in cats is a poor diet and the cumulative effect thereof. I have witnessed this firsthand and will share this experience in the next section.

As I mentioned in Chapter One, a dry-food-only diet is a health disaster waiting to happen. This is where cumulative effect comes in. Years and years of dry kibble slowly breaks down the integrity of the digestive system. It is constantly overworked, and eventually the immune system (80 percent of which is housed in the gut) gets sluggish and unknowingly allows pathogens into the body. The end result is disease.

A cat will eat approximately one cup of dry food daily, which is roughly 45 percent carbohydrates. Some brands contain a little more and some less. Once the food is hydrated from stomach fluids, this food becomes two cups in the gut, causing dehydration from within. Your cat would have to consume between eight and ten ounces of water daily just to keep from getting dehydrated. Most cats do not drink this much water on a daily basis, and that is where we run into health issues. It is imperative to keep a fresh clean supply of water available daily for your cat.

Another problem with commercial dry food is the cooking process. I had the opportunity to speak with a veterinary specialist with Hill's Science Diet in reference to the cooking process of their dry kibble. I was told that all the ingredients are mixed together in a huge vat. The mixture is then poured into a machine that pushes the mixture out through templates that are specifically designed for each type of food they sell. As it exits these templates, a knife-like machine cuts it off into kibbles. These kibbles are then dropped onto a conveyor belt that takes the food into a high-heat oven where it is baked. Most manufacturing pet food companies use this high-heat process to ensure the destruction of contaminants like bacteria, molds, fungus, or whatever else comes along. It is unfortunate that high heat also destroys most nutrients including vitamins, minerals, enzymes, and amino acids, specifically taurine. This process kills just about everything good in the food.

I asked the veterinary specialist at Hill's Science Diet how the company can ensure that the cat or dog is actually getting these nutrients, especially if they are being destroyed in the baking process. She said that she couldn't answer my question because she honestly didn't know. She did say that after the kibble is baked, it is sprayed with a palatable spray called their PALS spray. This is a flavor enhancer made from fats and vitamins C and E. As long as this spray has not been cooked or processed at high temperatures, at least these two nutrients are being added back in. I worry about the taurine and L-Carnitine as these two amino acids are crucial to the health of both dogs and cats. Blindness and heart problems can occur from a deficiency of these nutrients. This is why I add extra nutrients whenever I serve my zoo commercially prepared foods. I had a shepherd named Max that went blind at ten years of age rather suddenly, and my lab Jack has developed heart problems at the age of eleven. We know, hands down, that nutrition plays a vital role in the prevention of disease, so it is very important to make sure your pets are getting what they need nutritionally.

Kidney failure from years of consuming a poor diet can be corrected. I will give you my recommended protocol for kidney failure, but first I would like to share Samantha's story with you.

Samantha's Story—Kidney Failure

Samantha, an eight-pound gray tabby with piercing green eyes, refused to eat but was drinking constantly and seemed to continually urinate; she was very lethargic, and had lost weight. After several diagnostic tests the vet, Doc, determined that Samantha was in the beginning stages of renal failure and had a severe kidney infection. This meant that Samantha was in serious trouble. Her kidneys were no longer functioning as they should. I wondered how this could have happened. Samantha was only ten years of age.

Sam was an upstate New York rescue. At just six weeks of age, she was trapped down in the sewer pipes of the condo development where we lived. We actually got a construction worker to go spelunking through these twelve-inch pipes to get her out. My two shepherds were terrified of her when we brought her home, and she has ruled the roost ever since. Sewer Sam, as we called her, is a survivor, and I refused to face the possibility of her no longer being around. When she was a kitten, Michael and I would come home from work to find Sam hanging from the doorjambs with her nails stuck in the woodwork. We had no idea how long she'd been stuck there. One day we couldn't find her in the house at all, but after looking in all the closets and all the possible places that she could possibly hide, we discovered her lounging in the middle of the canopy of our bed. She had climbed the four-poster bed after using it as a scratch post and then snuggled down into the soft cotton canopy.

We couldn't train her not to climb, so we ended up declawing her for her own safety. This did not deter Sam from climbing. She learned to shimmy up the four-poster bed to her comfy spot. The only problem was she couldn't get down. After long deliberation we decided to have her back claws removed as well. I had a very tough time with this decision. We picked her up from the vet after surgery, and she seemed fine. At 2:00 a.m. the next morning we found her hemorrhaging and lying listless in the bathtub. An emergency room visit and four hundred dollars later, we took Sam home. After that day I vowed I would never declaw another cat again.

As an indoor-only cat, partially because of the declawing, Sam never had a desire for the great outdoors. But after her diagnosis of kidney failure, she just cried at the backdoor as if she wanted out. I figured if she was going to die anyway, what harm could it do to let her out? I often heard that when an animal is about to die, it will go off on its own somewhere to die alone. I wanted to let her do as she wished, so I opened the door and let her out. I followed her around the yard and noticed that she was sniffing the ground as if she were looking for something. When she found what she was searching for, she started eating the greens around her. Nothing in particular as far as I knew, but she seemed to know exactly what she wanted. After she finished, I waited for her to throw up as most cats often do after ingesting grass or plant matter, but this never happened. I brought her back inside, and this went on for the next several days. In the interim I researched an alternative approach to kidney failure in cats and immediately began introducing the recommended kidney support protocol to Samantha. I used this protocol combined with the knowledge I already knew about kidney failure in humans, and Sam rapidly showed signs of improvement.

I also researched the greens that Sam was eating in the backyard. I was able to identify two of the four plants that helped her recover from kidney failure. The first was dandelion leaves. Dandelion is an

Samantha

extremely medicinal weapon against kidney failure. It primarily acts as a diuretic and detoxifier aiding in the excretion of waste products through the kidneys. Dandelion is a great anti-inflammatory aid and useful in nephritis, which is inflammation of the kidney. The second plant that Sam chose was red clover, which is also known for its detoxifying effects, as well as being an anti-spasmodic. Red clover is great for anything that ails the urinary tract. It still amazes me that Sam knew instinctively what her body needed to heal itself.

I took her back to the vet the following week, and Doc was amazed at how great Sam looked. After repeating a blood panel, he determined that Sam was no longer in renal failure. When I told him what we did, he was amazed. This happened five years ago, and Samantha is still with us today, healthier then ever before. I must tell you that Samantha is primarily an outdoor cat now because she chooses to be, and she still rules the roost!

Protocol for Kidney Failure

The following are some very important foods, supplements, and guidelines for kidney failure.

- Greens (peas, red clover, dandelion leaves, spirulina, barley or wheat grass, or sea greens) provide chlorophyll, which is chock-full of antioxidant protection and beneficial nutrients such as amino acids, minerals, vitamins, enzymes, and carotene. Greens are touted for boosting immune function, detoxifying the body (especially red blood cells), and protecting cells from cancer-causing free radicals. Many of these greens can be juiced and added in small increments to wet food. The peas can be mashed and mixed into food, and the leaves should be snipped into small pieces and then added.
- Probiotics are essential to just about all illnesses or disorders. Probiotics aid digestion and kill harmful bacteria in the gut. They help to keep up the integrity of the digestive system and the immune system. Use as directed.
- B6 aids the body in ridding itself of excess water and also supports the balance between sodium and potassium. Administer 5–10 mg daily for a ten-pound cat.
- Vitamin C acidifies the urine, boosts immune function, and aids the healing process. Administer 100 mg daily.
- Cranberry capsules acidify the urine, destroy bacterial buildup, and promote healing of the urinary tract. Give ¼ of a capsule two times daily sprinkled on food (wet food preferably).
- Lecithin granules (plain) are used for inflammation of the kidneys and tissue repair. Increase energy levels and brain function. Administer ½ teaspoon daily added to food. Use as directed.
- Encourage the drinking of large amounts of water. You can do this by flavoring the water with tuna juice (no salt added and packed in water) or homemade chicken broth (no salt).

- Try to avoid a dry food diet, especially those that are high in protein. Wet food (organic) with added chopped greens, cranberry, mashed peas, and ½ teaspoon of lecithin granules is the best bet for kidney problems.

Leave fresh catnip and wheatgrass (cat grass) around the house in pots so that it is always available to your cat, especially if the great outdoors is not an option. It is also very important to eliminate as much stress in the household as possible as this can worsen any medical condition.

I would like to take a moment to update you on Pooh Bear's progress with his bacterial (pseudomonas) infection. After two weeks of probiotic nasal flushes, along with a product called colloidal silver added to his regime by adding a drop into each nostril twice daily, Pooh Bear finally beat this infection and was given a clean bill of health. After the use of antibiotic therapy using several antibiotics over several months failed, I resorted to these alternative therapies. For those of you who haven't heard of colloidal silver, it is a supplement with powerful healing properties. It has antifungal, antibiotic, and antiviral properties. Pooh Bear just turned one and is still pseudomonas free!

Cardiovascular Health

Cardiovascular disease affects cats as young as two years of age. A disease that used to be associated with older cats is now a threat to cats of all ages. This is a good protocol to follow whether your cat is sick, at high risk, or over the age of seven. It can also be used as a preventative measure. As mentioned before, I myself have lost two cats to cardiovascular disease. I wish I had known then what I know today about how to prevent heart disease. Maybe then I could have protected Baby and Silver. Because I covered heart disease in Chapter Three, I won't repeat myself in this section.

Taurine is extremely important where heart health is concerned. And because cat food manufacturers cannot guarantee that it is not destroyed during the cooking process, I believe it should be supplemented back into the diet. So this protocol begins with taurine.

Protocol for Heart Disease

Here is my recommended protocol for heart disease.

- Taurine is known to stabilize arrhythmia by sparing the loss of potassium from the heart muscle. It is also vital for proper utilization of sodium, potassium, calcium, and magnesium. Taurine also protects the brain. Supplement the diet with up to 125 mg of taurine daily. Taurine usually comes in capsules containing 500 mg. Pour ¼ of the capsule over your cat's food at least a few times a week.
- Coenzyme Q10 is a powerhouse supplement where heart disease is concerned. CoQ10 is an antioxidant, also called ubiquinone. It plays an intricate part in the production of energy in every cell in the body. Some of its actions include stimulating the immune system, aiding the circulatory system, increasing tissue oxygenation and fighting the aging process. The usual dosage for a ten-pound cat would be 10 mg daily. Oily fish, such as mackerel, salmon, and sardines, have the highest concentrations of CoQ10.
- Flaxseed oil is known for reducing pain and inflammation. It also reduces the hardening effects of cholesterol on cell membranes. Give ½ teaspoon daily mixed in wet food.
- Dandelion is a multifaceted herb that is useful in this protocol as well. If congestive heart failure occurs from fluid buildup in the lungs around the heart, this herb helps to reduce the stress on the heart from fluid overload. The conventional drug of choice would be Lasix to remove excess fluid.

- The Holistic Cat Immune-Boosting Formula—every nutrient in this formula supports heart health. Use as directed.
- Water—make sure there is plenty of fresh, clean water available for your cat, as dehydration will only place stress on the heart. Encourage drinking by adding tuna juice (no sodium added) or homemade chicken broth to the water, if necessary.
- Diet should be mostly canned food supplemented by a little bit of dry throughout the day. Remember that a dry food diet will dehydrate your cat and worsen her condition. Recommended supplements can be added directly to the wet food and mixed in. Snip fresh greens like dandelion and mix those in as well.
- Limit stressful situations such as frequent visits to the vet. A mobile veterinary service is a lot less stressful on your cat than bringing her to a set location. Most mobile vets will come to your home and see your pets on their (your pets') own turf. I would also recommend against regular grooming appointments if your cat has been diagnosed with heart disease. These can be very stressful.

Cardiomyopathy is a hard disease to reverse; however, it is my belief that you can maintain it and keep it from progressing with the heart health protocol just described.

Intestinal Health

The digestive system of a cat is very complex and extremely sensitive. Like ours, it includes the esophagus, stomach, duodenum, small intestine, large intestine (colon), rectum, and anus.

Cats suffer from many of the same ailments of the digestive tract that we do—things like constipation, diarrhea, stomach or intestinal viruses, gastritis (inflammation of the lining of the stomach), and even stomach ulcers.

Vomiting and diarrhea seem to be the two symptoms that cats suffer from the most. If your cat vomits clear or frothy fluid regularly, then it has most likely ingested bad food, grass, hair balls, foreign objects, or other indigestible things. It could also indicate certain intestinal viruses. A thick frothy yellow or bloody vomit could indicate a serious condition and you should seek medical assistance immediately. I usually don't try to stop vomiting as it is interfering with the body's natural response to getting rid of a problem. The most important thing to remember is that if your cat vomits repeatedly, then you must try to keep fluids readily available. This is because cats can rapidly become dehydrated from vomiting.

Cats can also get motion sickness from traveling by car, rail, or air. The over-the-counter drug Dramamine is well tolerated by cats. A ten-pound cat's dosage would be 12.5 mg and should be given at least an hour prior to departure. It is probably best not to feed your cat on the day you are traveling, as they do best traveling on an empty stomach.

Irritable Bowel Disease, or IBD, is on the rise in cats. I do feel this is primarily due to a poor diet, immunosuppression, and malnutrition. IBD simply means inflammation in the intestines. Here is Hope's story and her battle with IBD.

Hope's Story—Irritable Bowel Disease (IBD)

I had a cat named Hope that had to be outside or on the sunporch because her IBD was so bad. She would not even realize that she was defecating as she was walking around. She would use the litter box when she could get to one, but most times she would leave a trail. I knew that age had a lot to do with her problem as well as years of malnutrition. When Hope came into our lives, she was severely malnourished and weighed only four pounds. At one time she was a beautiful long-haired, bobtail, chocolate point Siamese. Hope was missing teeth and estimated to be fifteen-plus years of age when we found her.

Someone either dumped her (probably because of her IBD problem), or she wandered off and got lost. We found her in the woods, scared to death, near the colony of cats that we took care of. We took her to the veterinarian where she was diagnosed with IBD.

I learned to manage Hope's IBD for a few years with supplements and a special diet. She lived happily with us until she died in her sleep one night of old age. Hope was between eighteen and twenty years of age when she died.

Taking Hope completely off wheat and corn helped her immensely. We fed her a product called Solid Gold, which is a dry cat food without preservatives, dyes, additives, corn, wheat, or any other fillers. It is a great allergen-free food. At night she got my wet food concoction with added peas (for binding and phytonutrient power), probiotics, and digestive enzymes. Hope tolerated this diet very well.

Protocol for Intestinal Health

The cause of any ailments that affect intestinal health can be revealed by changing the diet first to see if that is the culprit, especially in cats with chronic diarrhea. So the following protocol begins with diet.

- If you completely change your cat's diet, it is imperative to do so gradually. Do this by beginning with a 3:1 ratio for the first week. For example, if you are giving your cat one cup of dry food daily, then use ¾ cup of her usual food mixed with ¼ cup of the new food. Look for organic, natural, free-range products. It is very important that they are allergen free, especially from wheat and corn. Natural Balance and Solid Gold are two very good brands.
- Probiotics would be the next step. Probiotics can be sprinkled over dry food or added to wet food. Remember that probiotics are essential in the treatment of just about all illnesses or disorders. Probiotics aid digestion and kill harmful bacteria in

the gut. They help to keep up the integrity of the digestive and immune systems. Use as directed.

- Digestive Enzymes—I use a product by PetGuard called Natural Digestive Enzyme Blend for Cats. It contains bromelain, amylase, cellulase, lipase, protease, phytase, alpha-galactosidase, acidophilus, bifidus, and calcium (to enhance uptake or absorption). PetGuard only uses human-grade ingredients in their pet products. This product, or digestive enzymes in general, assists the digestive system with the breakdown of food. Use as directed.

- The Holistic Cat Immune-Boosting Formula—because the digestive tract is compromised in IBD cats, it is imperative to support the immune system, which is housed in the digestive tract as we previously discussed. Use as directed.

- Flaxseed oil—½ teaspoon daily mixed in wet food. Essential fatty acids (flaxseed oil) are needed to protect the lining of the intestines as well as reduce inflammation.

- L-glutamine is an amino acid that is known for its healing properties in the gut. It aids the healing of ulcers and enteritis. L-glutamine should be taken with B6 and vitamin C for the best results. A great combination for intestinal health: 250 mg L-glutamine, 5 mg B6, and 100 mg vitamin C.

- Water—make sure there is an ample supply of fresh clean water available at all times. This is most important when cats eat a predominantly dry food diet.

I do not feel that steroids are the answer for cats with IBD. As noted, steroids like prednisone or prednisolone suppress immune function and set your cat up for a whole slew of other health problems (refer to Chapter Four). They truly only mask the symptoms of IBD.

Allergy/Skin Health

This protocol will be one of the most useful because most cats usually suffer from some sort of allergy problem at some point in their lives. Whether it's a food allergy, environmental allergy, or an allergy caused from flea bites, the body will react the same. It will recognize the invader (the allergen) and send out the troops (white cells) to try to overcome the offending pathogen. An allergy is simply an inappropriate response by the body's immune system to a substance that is not usually harmful. Typical symptoms of an allergic response are sneezing, nasal congestion, coughing, wheezing, itching, rash, fatigue, and headaches.

There are many allergens that can affect both humans and animals, and here are a few of the leading offenders for cats:

- Other animal dander, and some animals are even allergic to humans—our skin flakes off just as dander does and some animals, especially cats, can develop an allergy to us.
- Inhalants are the most common allergy in cats. Inhalants would include all pollen, dust, molds, and mildew. Even if you have indoor cats, they can still be affected by pollen. Household dust can pose a problem for your cat because it is so prevalent. Weekly dusting and vacuuming will help keep dust mites down. Molds can also be a problem because they too can live throughout the house, under sinks and in closets, basements, laundry rooms, and even outside in the air and soil. Molds like damp dark places. Inhalant allergies usually exhibit symptoms similar to hay fever, although itching is also a common symptom when dealing with inhalant allergies.
- Some foods, such as chicken, fish, beef, wheat, corn, dairy, and even eggs, can cause an allergic reaction in cats. Some experts advise continually rotating your cat's diet. For example, if you feed your cat canned food, give her a variety, not

just fish or turkey or beef. Vary the flavors so your cat won't build up an intolerance to any one food. The same with dry food. You can stay within your brand but use different flavors periodically.

- Drugs—cats have allergies to drugs just like we do. Observe your cat closely anytime she is on medication.

Protocol for Allergy

Because cats in general can be allergic to so many things, my protocol begins with probiotics for maximum immune health.

- Probiotics aid digestion and kill harmful bacteria in the gut. They help to keep up the integrity of the digestive system and the immune system. Use as directed.
- Digestive enzymes assist the digestive system with the breakdown of food and help the body to reduce inflammation. Use as directed.
- Flaxseed oil reduces inflammation and is good for relieving itching and symptoms associated with allergies. Flaxseed can benefit every system in the body. Give ½ teaspoon daily mixed in cat food.

OR

- Fish oil is also great for all conditions of the skin, especially those associated with allergies. Cats and dogs can both benefit from this product. Fish oil is an excellent source of omega-3 fatty acids. You must purchase a reputable brand such as Nordic Naturals or Carlson Labs. A cheaper brand may result in contaminants such as parasites, bacteria, or mercury. Fish oil must be molecularly distilled. Use ½ teaspoon daily.
- Garlic—use the odorless capsule form of garlic in minute amounts mixed into wet food to aid sinus inflammation, boost

immune function, and fight off offending pathogens. Use one quarter of a capsule per ten-pound cat.

- Diet should be varied as I just mentioned. Make sure you choose an allergen-free food and stay within your brand, or you may cause stomach upset. Just rotate the flavors. Adding some greens will also help by boosting immune function with phytonutrient power.

Dealing with allergies can be extremely frustrating. Have patience and try to eliminate or at least manage all possible allergens in your cat's environment. Weekly cleaning, keeping windows closed, and keeping your cat inside during hay fever season should help.

I want to take a few minutes to talk about ringworm. Ringworm is a very tenacious fungus. It was appropriately named because of the scaly red ring that forms with an infection of ringworm. In cats this fungus doesn't always form a ring; instead, it will form red scaly patches with hair loss. Hair loss is oftentimes the telltale sign that ringworm is present. Ringworm tends to affect immune-suppressed kittens and cats, although healthy cats can also get ringworm if stressed or out of sorts. We, as a rescue, have endured many cases of ringworm. Some cats will blow it off fairly easily, but others will fight the infection for six to eight weeks.

I have successfully treated mild ringworm infections holistically using tea tree oil spray by Desert Essence. This spray, applied to the affected area three times daily, will clear up the infection in a couple of weeks. I also use the immune-boosting formula added to food to enhance the healing process. For a more tenacious infection, I resort to Griseofulvin, an antifungal/antibiotic prescription medication. I usually have it compounded into a fish- or liver-tasting liquid for the cats. This works extremely well, and in two to three weeks the infection is gone. You can usually tell when ringworm has been defeated by new hair growth in the area of the infection. Lily, a woman who needed our assistance as a rescue, had a litter of five adorable kittens

Lily's Kittens

that had been abandoned by their mother. I bottle-fed them from the time they were two weeks old. They had an extremely bad case of ringworm, and the only thing that cleared it up was the Griseofulvin. However, I did have to wait until they were four weeks of age to treat them. Gus and Christopher were orange tabbies, and Lily, Cami, and Maggie were all white calicos. Cami ended up passing away from fading kitten syndrome, but the other four thrived and eventually went to good homes.

FINAL WORD

With proper care and a safe environment, your cat should live to a ripe old age. Our cats rely on us, their guardians, to protect them, care for them, and, most of all, love them. Cats are extremely affectionate creatures and will be faithful companions till the end, if treated well.

To keep your cat healthy, he or she should have:

- A healthy, balanced diet consisting of both wet and dry food, including vegetables and omega-3 in the form of flaxseed oil or fish oil.
- Plenty of fresh clean water.
- Supplements for immune support to be given as needed.
- Limited use of pharmaceutical medications—only when necessary. Vaccines should be given as needed and not given needlessly or on an annual basis. Dangerous vaccines such as the leukemia vaccine should be avoided.
- A safe environment free from harmful cleaners, plants, and other toxic materials or substances.
- Plenty of room to exercise and an array of toys or kitty trees to keep him or her occupied and free from boredom.

A cat should be able to visit the outside world. Safe ways to do this are:

- A fenced-in yard.
- A screened-in sun room.
- A kittywalk tunnel leading outside to an enclosure.
- Periodic walks on a leash.
- Supervised outings.

Never allow your cat to roam. Always know where your cat is. Danger lurks where you can't protect him or her. Cars, other animals, people, and poisons lie in wait for your cat.

When relocating or planning a trip, be sure to follow the protocols recommended. And remember that cats have feelings just like we do. Depression, jealousy, and anger are all emotions that cats experience. When you introduce a new pet into the household, remember to pay extra special attention to your cat. Don't give him or her the opportunity to express bad emotions and behaviors. Whether you are moving, traveling, or introducing a new pet, these transitions should not be difficult and should be non-threatening to your cat.

When your cat is faced with illness, keep in mind that the protocols contained within this book are strictly for guidance and can be used in the event that you cannot get medical attention; however, a cat with a life-threatening illness should always be seen by a veterinarian.

I hope this book has helped you to enrich and prolong the life of your cat. Education cures ignorance, and without ignorance all things are possible. May you and your cat have a happy, healthy life!

Bluebell

References and Reading Material

Balch, Phyllis A. 2006. *Prescription for Nutritional Healing*. 4th ed. New York: Avery / Penguin Putnam.

Carlson, Delbert G. and James M. Giffin. 1995. *Cat Owner's Home Veterinary Handbook*. New York: Howell Book House.

Hamilton, Don. 1999. *Homeopathic Care for Cats and Dogs: Small Doses for Small Animals*. Berkeley: North Atlantic Books.

Hatherill, J. Robert. 1999. *Eat To Beat Cancer: A Research Scientist Explains How You and Your Family Can Avoid Up to 90% of All Cancers*. Riverside, CA: Renaissance Books.

Hendrick M.J., Goldschmidt M.H., Sofer F.S., Wang Y.Y., Somlyo A.P. 1992. Postvaccinal sarcomas in the cat: epidemiology and electron probe microanalytical identification of aluminum. *Cancer Research* 52 (19): 5391–4.

Kahn, Cynthia M., ed. 2005. *The Merck Veterinary Manual*. 9th ed. Duluth, GA: Merial Limited.

Kidd, Randy. 2000. *Dr. Kidd's Guide to Herbal Cat Care*. Pownal, VT: Storey Books.

Kirk, Robert W. 1992. *Small Animal Practice (Current Veterinary, Therapy XI)*. 11th ed. Ed. John D. Bonagura, 205. San Diego, CA: Harcourt.

Martins, Ann N. 1997. *Food Pets Die For: Shocking Facts about Pet Food*. Troutdale, OR: New Sage Press.

Pottenger, Francis Marion. 1995. *Pottenger's Cats: A Study in Nutrition*. Lemon Grove, CA: Price-Pottenger Nutrition Foundation.

Rainbolt, Dusty. 2004. *Kittens for Dummies*. Indianapolis, IN: Wiley Publishing.

Springhouse Nurse's Drug Guide 2005. 2004. Philadelphia: Lippincott Williams & Wilkins.

Holistic Pet Food Companies

Artemis Company—provides not only wholesome pet food but also a whole-life approach to treating animals. Visit their Web site at http://www.artemiscompany.com.

Feline Instincts—provides a natural pet food based on raw meat. Visit their Web site at http://www.felineinstincts.com.

Natura—an organic pet food company dedicated to making the best pet food available. Visit their Web site at http://www.naturapet.com.

Newman's Own Organics—premium pet food that uses only natural antioxidant preservatives. Visit their Web site at http://www.newmansownorganics.com.

Only Natural Pet Store—provides a huge selection of natural pet supplies and food. Visit their Web site at http://www.only-naturalpet.com.

Pet Wellness Companies

BlackKat Herbs—pet supplies, including homeopathics, herbal remedies, natural food, and diatomaceous earth. Visit their Web site at http://www.blackkatherbs.com.

Holistic Animal Medicines—the naturopathic pharmacy for animals and world's largest supplier of natural animal formulas. Visit their Web site at http://www.holisticanimalmedicines.com.

Woodland Natural Remedies—natural holistic veterinary remedies for dogs and cats. Visit their Web site at http://www.woodland-naturalremedies.com.

Cat Fences and Enclosures

Just 4 Cats—a safe cat enclosure company that stocks over sixty-five drawings of cat enclosures. Visit their Web site at http://www.just4cats.com.

Purr...fect Fence—specializing in safe, durable cat fencing and enclosures. Visit their Web site at http://www.purrfectfence.com.

The Cat's Den—provides outdoor cat enclosures, window cat enclosures, playpens, and safe containments for cats. Visit their Web site at http://www.thecatsden.net.

Supplement Companies for Cats

Long Life Supplements—natural pet supplements that are individualized for specific diseases. Visit their Web site at http://www.longlifesupplements.org.

Precious Pets—a company that offers natural supplements for cats and dogs. For more information, visit their Web site at http://www.preciouspets.org.

Purely Pets—pet nutrition at its finest. Offering natural vitamins and supplements for cats. Visit their Web site at http://www.purelypets.com.

Web sites cited:

www.cdc.gov/drugresistance
www.fda.gov
www.ISARonline.org.legislation
www.ncbi.nlm.nih.gov
www.novaccines.com

About the Author

Jennifer A. Coscia, NC, an internationally recognized nutritional consultant specializing in disease prevention, combined her background in nutrition for humans with her love for and care of animals to found The Animal Rescue and Adoption Agency, Inc., a non-profit (501c3) no-kill organization for the betterment of animal welfare. As a Petco partner, she has rescued and placed hundreds of homeless pets into loving homes.

An accomplished journalist and the author of *The Fat Elimination and Detox Program: A Holistic Approach to Weight-loss and Disease Prevention,* Coscia has written for several health publications including *Natural Awakenings* magazine, *The Beaches* magazine, and *The San Marco News*. She is a popular guest speaker and workshop leader for several health organizations, including The American Cancer Society and The Lymphoma Society.

Coscia is a certified consultant for Dr. Peter D'Adamo's Blood Type Diet and the *Eat Right For Your Blood Type* series and has facilitated educational courses on nutrition for the Internal Medicine Department at Shands Hospital at the University of Florida. As a specialist in Holistic Nutrition, she has appeared on FOX TV's mini health series *What the Doctors Don't Tell You* and has been interviewed about health topics by First Coast News Channel 12. Coscia lives in Jacksonville, Florida.